TWIN JOUR⎯.
the soul and the personality

Sue Vickers Tordoff

Sue Vickers Tordoff

Photos © 2021 Sue Vickers Tordoff
Diagram illustrations by Stephen Pelling

Contents

Sue Vickers Tordoff: Professional Qualifications
Background

Twin Journeys

The aim in writing this book is to keep the integrity of the material while making it user-friendly, so that it can be applied to everyday life, a simple introduction to the two journeys.

Introduction

This is an account of the twin journeys of the soul and the personality, built on an evolving framework as our understanding changes and we perceive more about the relationship between psychology, religion/belief and philosophy. At times these strands may intertwine, become inseparable. At other times it is useful to separate them in order to enhance our perception. There is a value in both.

Just as your week may begin on Sunday and mine on Monday, so we may see our journeys beginning differently. And just as the days of the week are continuous, in a sense not bound by beginning and endings except by man's framework, so I would suggest are our journeys continuous. However, we need a starting point, as we are viewing it from the plane where boundaries are important. In our present perspective, birth is seen as the beginning and that seems appropriate, although we may have to go back before birth to explore roles of father/mother as the soul approaches physical birth.

The Soul's Journey

The soul exists before the personality, on a Higher Plane variously described as Heaven or the Soul Plane etc. Whatever the name ascribed to this place or plane, it appears in almost all the major religious beliefs as a place of unity, of true connection with other beings, of openness of communication and response, of God or the Supreme Being. For reasons we shall explore, the soul's journey to incarnation on the Earth plane necessitates leaving behind this total connection, though the sense of it may remain.

We are carried in our mother's womb for nine months, completely protected and literally at one with our mother. For some beings, this unity continues for many months after birth, with a slowly growing awareness of separateness, that indeed we are not part of the mother, but a being in our own right.

As we make progress in life, assuming we are seeking spiritual and psychological growth and wholeness, we begin to experience connectedness again, in new ways.
The purpose of the Soul is to gather and experience many facets of earthly existence. The sum total of this learning will eventually be fed back to the Soul Group, like a family, of which it is part.

The Personality's Journey

When a soul journeys to the Earth plane for incarnation in a human body, it needs protection to cope with the denser atmosphere, and skills in order to live and relate on this plane. It develops around itself a personality, a unique collection of characteristics and abilities. Parents, and those with parental responsibilities for a child, influence personality development and growth to some extent. Anyone taking on the task of caring for and rearing a child takes on important psychological and spiritual work. Those seeking to understand their own particular personality and spiritual framework face a continuation of this work. We can choose to ignore everything related to this, but even that choice is part of the journey and sooner or later, on the Earth plane or another, we will have to look at what that choice means.

The Twin Journeys

One complete cycle of our journey necessitates leaving connectedness and unity, experiencing separateness and then journeying back again to unity. To be more explicit: pre-conception, conception, birth transition, life during incarnation, death transition and post death or reunion with spirit. This involves both psychological and spiritual connections, and our growth depends partly on how we handle connections and separations throughout life. Each one of us at some stage has to deal with rejection (even abandonment), with attachment that is either appropriate or not, with clinging on to and with letting go. Throughout all this, our relationship – or lack of it – with Spirit or God or the Source is paramount in how we manage our journeys. If we begin integration between psychological and spiritual growth, we are doing very well indeed.

Many of the themes addressed here defy nutshell definition and would benefit from a book in themselves. All would reward further specialised study. My aim is to create a simple introduction to the subjects, to bring together the spiritual and psychological strands to weave a life journey that makes better sense than either strand on its own.

From this brief introduction to this huge field of study and learning, it's easy to see how words might get in the way. Words carry an emotional charge, different for each of us. Each person reading this will have their own perspective, their framework of belief and their own anathemas. I could litter the text with alternative either/or words in an effort to please everyone, but doubtless I would still upset or even disaffect others. Likewise, use of 'man' or 'mankind' is a shorthand term for the whole of humanity and includes both men and women. If you are at all interested in learning how to be a spiritual parent or in putting your own growth in perspective, and you find a word sticking in your throat or gut, try substituting a word nearest your own viewpoint and see where it takes you. In the interests of clarity, therefore, Appendix 1 has a list of definitions of the way I have used some words.

I recommend reading one chapter at a time, giving yourself opportunity to digest and assimilate what it means for you. Knowledge alone is not enough; you have to feel it, taste it, know it in your heart as well as your mind. Grasping at concepts will bring only short-term benefits. Gradual incorporation into daily life brings lasting benefits and wisdom.

The whole story of the Twin Journeys is based on my years of personal study, learning, gaining counselling and healing qualifications and experience of working with clients and groups. I am particularly indebted to teachers Mary Cox, Ruth White, Barbra Somers and Ian Gordon Brown (see Appendix 2) for imparting over the years, their knowledge and understanding with such care and wisdom. While benefitting from their theories and teaching, this work is the result of my own personal conclusions. Any errors in interpretation are therefore my own.

Sue Vickers Tordoff

Twin Journeys

Chapter 1
Pre-Birth

In our society at present there seems to be a move towards specialism, towards breaking down into small areas of knowledge, and devolving regions of the world. While this may be a desirable breaking away from over-paternalistic states of country and mind, we do not want lose sight of the whole picture.

This seems to be a good time to explore the dual journeys we make on this earth plane, that of the soul and that of the personality. Often, they are looked at separately by those with vested interests in separating out these parts, and indeed it may be necessary to do that in order to deepen our understanding. Bringing the two together however, seeing them as an intertwined whole, can illumine the difficulties and setbacks we face and give meaning to our lives.

For this exploration I am assuming that the reader has some familiarity with the concept of reincarnation. One cycle of incarnation – from inception through conception, birth, growing to adulthood and death – will be covered, with particular emphasis on the birth process as the first transition.

Briefly, reincarnation is a belief that a soul descends from the soul plane, inhabits a human body for a life span and then returns to the soul plane for rest, assessment and recuperation before preparation for another incarnation. The process is continuous and some belief systems state that a soul can make several hundred incarnations before attaining nirvana, the desired state of enlightenment or illumination, when the soul may choose to make no further human incarnations. An incarnation is a single cycle in this process.

Inherent in the theory of reincarnation is the system of karma. Karma has been much misunderstood in the west; so often it is presented as a tit-for-tat system of revenge and retribution. I suggest it is a much more self-regulating mechanism. The biblical phrase 'as ye sow, so shall ye reap' – or the current version 'what goes around, comes around' – is fairly apt. Any action attracts a response, a negative action attracts a like response, a positive action attracts a positive response. In simplistic terms, you get back what you give out.

Contrary to common belief, karma does not necessarily involve a response to the same person in successive lifetimes. In both the psychological and spiritual journey, we can work out original issues with different people, within an incarnation as well as in succeeding incarnations. Some issues are so complex they become themes for several lifetimes.

The purpose of incarnating on earth is to gain experience not available on other planes of existence. For instance, the lower planes including this one, are the only planes where clashes occur – personality differences, violence, hatred, anger, what we might think of as emotions with a darker tinge. We have divisions between people that are unknown on higher planes of experience and existence. The aim of each incarnation is to gather experience, processing it, learning through it, eventually transmuting it into wisdom.

Some belief systems liken incarnations to going to school. The more we learn, the more we progress through school. We no longer have to go back to the intake class, and though lessons may have to be repeated, they are generally of a higher order, a similar learning but at a higher level.

There is a spiral effect to learning; imagine the view of a landscape from low on the spiral. You can learn much from that view, but any ridge will block out further aspects. If you go higher up the spiral, you can see beyond the ridge, and more information will be available to you for processing.

In the same way that we belong to families on the earth plane, so we belong to groups of souls on the higher plane. Each group will have what we would call a characteristic, a vibration, that it works with easily. People belonging to this group might not follow the same career or be in the same earthly family, but will have similar leanings, a similar belief structure. As we progress through incarnations and gain experience with spiritual work as well as work here on earth, we may begin to recognise other people who we describe as kindred spirits. We may say we are on the same wavelength.

In between incarnations, each soul is 'debriefed'. The group will have, amongst its members, teachers and more advanced beings who are there to help the newly returned soul. There will be a review of the life just lived; in simple terms, the soul is encouraged to look at what happened with discernment rather than judgement, how he/she handled situations, the effects of life choices, and if things could have been done differently. In addition, the accumulated experience and knowledge is gathered into the store for that particular soul group. Each incarnation, therefore, furthers both personal and collective growth.

An assessment *is made by the soul* in conjunction with its helpers, the degree of autonomy depending on the state of advancement. There is no judgement other than our own discernment. Periods of rest, recuperation, healing, counselling, any help needed, follow as necessary. More learning may be necessary before the next incarnation. Whatever it takes to further the soul's development is given consideration and help.

13

There may be opportunities to work in particular areas of interest, on the spiritual plane.

In due time, the soul will be ready for the next incarnation, again a decision is taken in consultation with guides and helpers. Much will now be considered; the last few lifetimes, lessons learnt or those which went unheeded, gaps or lacks in experience and knowledge, the sum total of all the particular soul has experienced so far, the gender and conditions needed for the next span of learning.

During all this time, the soul has lived in harmony with its fellow beings on the higher or soul plane. Now it is ready to return to the earth plane, the process must be gradual, allowing the sensitive 'pure' soul time to acclimatise and prepare itself for the rigours of life on earth.

The soul is guided to approach the earth plane, focussing on parents whose own learning and circumstances fit the chosen pattern. Childbearing and raising is a mutual learning process for parents and children. Despite the apparent situation in some cases, the soul aspect of future parents will have indicated a willingness to birth a child as part of their incarnation pattern. Other conditions considered might involve, for example, poverty, wealth, skills, race, geographical location, gender and many other areas of particular learning, and can also include congenital hereditary disability in an extreme case. The emphasis is on learning with choice, not punishment for some past misdeeds or 'bad' karma.

One or both parents will have been forming an etheric web or mesh, a spiritual environment created from intention and desire to have a child, or from their love for each other. If these conditions do not exist, the web will grow from the knowledge of the pregnancy, and perhaps from the pre-incarnation willingness of the soul of the parent to birth a child. The etheric web is a kind of holding area, denser than the conditions the soul is used to, but less dense than the earth plane. It is necessary to adjust slowly to the 'heavier' vibrations of earth.

The gradual coming closer to this plane is necessary for other reasons too; the steady letting go of the spirit plane, and of what we would call memory. Awareness of past lives drops away as the soul nears the earth plane. Disturbing flotsam from many incarnations might confuse present learning if it surfaced too early. All of this enables the soul to come close to the parents and to the earth plane, to acclimatise gradually before the moment when it enters the foetus, unencumbered by knowledge of former lives.

The foetuses of miscarriages, terminations and still-born babies will all have been held in the etheric web, will all have experienced the closeness of the parent(s) and the earth plane vibrations. For some, it will have been enough to come close this time around, to dip a toe in the water. A traumatic previous life could necessitate such a cautious approach to this incarnation, not unlike learning to walk again after an accident or stroke. There will be learning for the soul (though not, perhaps, for the personality which didn't have time to form) in each of these experiences.

It is a matter of scholarly and esoteric debate as to the actual moment when the soul enters the foetus. It may be when the heart starts to beat, or when the foetus 'quickens'. It may be at the moment of first breath that the soul moves from the etheric web and truly merges with the foetus, it may be earlier. In some ways it is academic; the soul is near enough (in our terms) certainly during the latter half of the pregnancy to hear and experience events around the mother, vibrations conducted along the etheric web. The key is that by or at the moment of birth, the soul is part of the new-born child.

Looked at from this perspective, we can already see the importance of parenting work. It is spiritual work of a high order. Fortunately, we are now beginning to rediscover this aspect of birthing in Western Culture.

Chapter 2
Birth

Picture the soul nearing our earth plane, like a child preparing to go back to school. The soul is coming to incarnation as a learning experience, with previous karma to work out and positive karma to build up. There will be vulnerability in entering the denser atmosphere of this plane.

The incoming soul doesn't have memories of past experience to help or hinder; each incarnation starts afresh. Some belief systems call the incoming soul the 'pure seed' for this reason. It is important to appreciate that the soul is whole and can only ever be whole. It is also important to remember that though certain experiences and learning are deemed desirable in this incarnation, there is no life-plan that must be adhered to, no prescription. Although there are guidelines for each life, determined as we have seen by the soul with advice and guidance, the soul has free choice. Life choices and their results will be considered after the incarnation.

The soul has started to become acclimatised to earth vibrations, to the vibrations of its mother and to some extent to her surroundings. The mother's physical condition and the food she eats, whether she smokes or takes alcohol or drugs, obviously affects the physical condition of the foetus. A lot of research has been done to show that what happens to the mother while she is pregnant impacts the foetus psychologically too. This will be explored in Chapter 3, the Birth Story.

The vulnerable soul merging with the foetus is ready to be born into our world. We have become more sensitive to the needs of the birthing mother in the last few decades, but the wider practice is still to give birth in hospital, in clinical surroundings with brilliant lights, and multiplicity of sights and sounds. In some instances, a Caesarian section has been routinely recommended for convenience rather than medical necessity. Birth is therefore a traumatic transition for the soul, newly entered into a physical body which is being squeezed and pushed from its warm moist dark safe place into this often discordant and harsh atmosphere.

To live on earth, for the soul to cope with the barrage of stimuli, it needs protection. The personality forms such protection around the soul, and the parents are responsible for protecting the emerging and developing soul-personality. The mother generally has the more immediate responsibility, though not always.

The development of the personality is based on several facets: the soul's true essence, what has gone before to a certain extent, genes from the parents, and the conditions obtaining during its development. So although born a pure seed, an innocent, it is not entirely a blank page. Innate skills, knowledge, experience and wisdom can all be re-accessed, depending on conditions, opportunities and the maturity of the soul. The personality is part of a complex process of evolution. It clothes the soul for the duration of its stay on the denser earth plane.

Child development is a huge (and thorny!) subject. An outline will suffice for our purposes, showing the relationship with the soul. All references here are to an ideal process of development. Potential pitfalls will be covered in Chapter 3. For further reading on the psychology of child development, see Appendix 2.

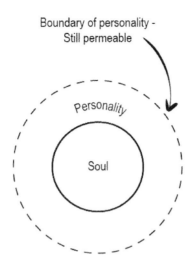

Diag. 1
'pure seed' at birth with emerging personality

Having been held in the mother-father created ethereal web and having been part of the mother, the soul-personality has to cope with the sudden physical separation from its mother. For some time after birth, it believes itself to be still a part of the mother, to identify them both as a single unit. It is her responsibility to provide protection in the form of boundaries while the personality develops. The boundary of the incipient personality is shown in Diagram 1 as a dotted line, permeable, allowing exchanges in and out, to and from the soul. If that level of openness were to continue as the child grew to adulthood, it would – unless the soul is extremely mature and developed – be harmful. Too many harsh vibrations, vastly over stimulated, the soul would not thrive and go through the incarnation with the ability to learn and experience. The experience of this highly necessary maternal protection means that the baby for a while has no concept of Other. It is one with the mother.

Mother's Role

Baby

Diag 2-1

In Diagram 2-1, the mother's arms around the newly born is symbolic of her protection on different levels; not only on the obvious physical level, but also on the psychological level as we have seen, while the personality forms and firms up, and further, on a spiritual level. Because of the openness of the soul, the baby needs protection from any harmful influences or negative vibrations, and the mother automatically provides this. Holding, cradling the baby gives comfort on all these levels, soothing, offering safety, nurturing. On leaving the close confines of the womb, touch and holding are needed as well as food and drink to produce a healthy thriving child.

As the eyes begin to focus, the baby perceives the world around by sight as well as sound, which was already developed in the womb. Touch, paramount from the moment of birth, is a two-way thing, the need to be touched and the need to touch in order to explore.

Baby forming
own personality

Diag. 2-2

Diagram 2-2 shows the soul with the developing personality, and the mother still providing all the protection and boundary. The baby effectively does not know where it begins and ends.

Bodily sensation develops, the experience of being able to wiggle toes, wave limbs. In the first year, the child has examined its fingers and toes and begins to have a sense of its extremities, though still closely linked with the mother. It begins to sit up unaided. It will have examined by sight and touch mother's face and come to know it, and many other things. During this time the mother's task is to demonstrate how safe she can make the baby and to affirm the baby's sense of itself. The parent(s) and others around play a valuable part in helping the child discover that he is a separate person. The old game of covering your eyes with your hands and gradually emerging to say 'peek-a-boo' to the child, or encouraging the child to do likewise is actually a crucial way of saying 'I see you'. The child needs to be seen as an individual in order to see itself as a being separate from the mother. Independence is a long way ahead, but this first realisation is, I believe, the beginning of what Jung called individuation, the process of integrating life's learning and experience, and a journey towards wholeness of being. See Appendix 1 Definitions.

Baby getting ready
to move out

Diag. 2-3

When the child starts to crawl and then takes its first staggering steps, the mother opens her arms a little wider, but holds them there ready to catch the child, closing them immediately danger threatens. Thus the child is encouraged to develop a sense of self by developing independent motion while keeping certain knowledge that the arms are still there.

By the age of 2-3, the child has discovered where it ends, which means it is beginning to know that mother and father, perhaps siblings, are Other, and the child starts to identify itself as 'I'. The ego is formed, the personality is becoming defined. It knows its own boundaries ready for the next step into the world. But the child is still the centre of its own universe.

Going to play group around this age helps the development of the sense of Others, especially if there are no siblings. Others have needs to be satisfied too. There are toys and attention to be shared. The child may still be the centre of its own universe, but it is becoming aware that others may have their turn in the centre.

Child beginning
to face the world

Diag. 2-4

The mother helps this process by opening her arms wider and leaving the child for short spells in the company of others. The child functions as an individual for the first time in this way, though still needing responsible Others to safeguard and help. The personality has been firming up through this process, the boundary becomes less permeable.

Father's Role

Diag. 3-1

In Diagram 3-1, the role of the father is illustrated. His arms surround both mother and child, providing an umbrella of safety and security. He traditionally has had roles in the outer world which are a necessary part of his physical provision for his family. Ideally in addition, psychologically he underpins the development of his child's personality, and spiritually underpins the provision of boundaries. In these ways, he supports the mother's task. He provides a safety net, a second set of boundaries as the soul finds the personality structure for this lifetime.

The World

Diag. 3-2

At a certain point, both mother and father can gradually reduce their protection while the child moves into the wider world.

In today's society, not all families have the old traditional structure of support. Psychologically we know that both men and women have qualities traditionally known as masculine and feminine. Stereotypes have arisen out of historical factors concerning survival. Today we are not bound by having to survive in the wild, and both men and women are free to express qualities formerly associated with the other gender. A parent of either sex is therefore not necessarily vital to the child's development, but two parents are still preferable to one, to share the tasks as we have seen. From the kind of support described already, it's easy to see that one person – trying to fulfill all the functions in the outer world, in the home and in the inner worlds of psyche and soul – could become seriously overstretched. Often for single parents, financial survival takes up the most time. Everything else has to fall into place behind that. It is the equivalent of the old hunting-gathering activities; without it the family fails to thrive, may even fail to survive. What has the single parent left in reserve to provide the necessary psychological and spiritual boundaries?

This is not a criticism of single parent families, nor an attack on any lifestyle. It is simply stating the obvious fact that with too many tasks falling to one person it becomes an enormous undertaking to do them well without become depleted. In Chapter 7, we see it is certainly possible to do the work of child rearing 'well enough'.

While necessarily striving to survive physically, the single parent may become impoverished spiritually and psychologically. We have to look elsewhere for our sustenance, ways of sustaining ourselves. Care-sharing with an ex- or with a friend can alleviate the difficulties, but more awareness of the kind of tasks involved is needed. Or Grandparents often play a vital part in supplying some of the boundaries, where there is geographical closeness and indeed, where there is enough emotional trust for the single parent to allow grandparents to fulfill some of the functions. Their wisdom and role as a second support network can be a valuable contribution. The roles do not have to be assigned in the old male-female way, but they do have to be fulfilled if we are to have a healthy society.

To further elucidate some of the points in this chapter. The personality is a valuable part of our learning and protection. It allows us to live on earth, to make relationships in a way not possible on other planes, to have intimate sexual exchanges, to clash with other beings, to earn a living, to educate ourselves and above all, to learn. It gives us a vehicle along with the physical body to partake if we wish in the spiritual work of procreation, helping other souls come into incarnation, and it allows us to undertake whatever spiritual work we choose on this plane. Think of inspirational leaders like Martin Luther King, Billy Graham, or workers for the good of humanity like Mother Theresa and Gandhi. Their physical bodies and personalities were part of the reason they could do the work, giving them presence, allowing them a conduit from Spirit, God or the higher plane in order to reach people.

A final note of caution. There are certain 'spiritual' cults and creeds which advocate the transcending of the personality and/or body. In context of the above, it will be seen that this is no easy task to be undertaken lightly. It is spiritual work of the utmost seriousness and magnitude, and only possible by souls advanced in learning, who have incarnated perhaps many hundreds of times. To attempt such transcendence without resolving issues of the personality – through psychological growth and understanding – and without experiencing long spiritual training under guidance, is to incur inevitable and possibly severe psychological problems. We have seen the role the personality plays in protection and growth. Discarding this without thorough preparation and guidance is a risky exercise.

Chapter 3
Birth Story

The process of birth is the first major transition of each incarnation as the soul moves from spirit into matter, from the soul plane to the earth plane. The importance of the quality of this experience is easily overlooked, and so I include here a short exploration of the birth story.

The facts about the birth of the individual are often obscured by family lore, by later conditioning or due to lapse of memory of the mother and those present at the birth. Nevertheless, birth remains the primary experience of the individual life, and the individual has ideas about the event. The term 'birth story' is used here to indicate the pre-natal history and birth experience, *whether real or imagined*, of the individual. Whatever an individual believes about his or her birth has relevance and sets the scene for future life transitions.

Because of the unknown and sometimes unknowable nature of the subject, we might look to myth, in particular the personal myth, as a way of approaching the pre-verbal experience.

A word of explanation. The importance of myth to psychological understanding has long been recognised in certain schools of psychology, eg. Jungian and Transpersonal. Myth traditionally carries the past into the present, in the form of the accumulated wisdom of a culture. It also attempts to explain the inexplicable; phenomena for which there are few or no historical or scientific explanations have been explained symbolically in myth. One example could be our creation myths, handed down originally by word of mouth.

All myths contain archetypal figures (eg. the hero) and qualities (eg. courage). Archetypes are deep and abiding patterns which remain potent and present in the traditional stories of all cultures as well as in the inner world of the individual. You might think of some of the characters – the Wicked Step Mother, the Handsome Prince, the Maiden in Distress. And abiding qualities such as Peace, War, Love and Wisdom. Characters and qualities in these stories touch us, some more deeply than others, because of the make-up of individual personalities.

Why would we need a 'personal myth'? The term has been used by Jung to describe the whole life story. Mythology, with its symbols and images, is the language which comes closest to the natural workings of the psyche, and the personal myth explains the individual's world in the way that cultural myths carry out that function for society.

Experience at birth is relevant to later well-being, and each of us may give our birth some meaning far more significant than mere fact. Arthur Janov, in his work on primal therapy, suggests that although we may not remember birth events themselves, they are nevertheless registered in our unconscious and in our bodies. He writes about 'imprints', a special category of memory he describes as repressed memories which find their way into the body and produce distorted organic and psychological functions, i.e. some illnesses such as migraine and some fears and phobias such as claustrophobia, though there is no evidence to prove that *all* such illnesses and fears have their beginnings in this way.

Other studies show the importance to the unborn child of events, both physical and emotional, in the life of the mother during pregnancy. We have seen how the soul comes close to the earth plane and to the parents during the pre-birth stage; as its senses adjust and develop, it is open to sounds and sensations occurring to and in close proximity to the mother. It is a possibility that the mother's feelings and thoughts are woven into the emotional fabric of the unborn child. This poses the question: does two-way empathic resonance occur in utero i.e. from mother to baby as well as from baby to mother, and if so, what is its significance? There is much still to research and learn in this area. We have barely scratched the surface here, enough to think of it as a possibility.

Influences after birth are well documented in many theoretical frameworks, for example in script theory of Transactional Analysis (see Appendix 1), and in these frameworks there is often debate about the moment of onset of such influences or script issues, similar to the debate about the moment the soul enters the foetus.

I see the birth story, as defined above, as the beginning of the personal myth. As such, it may provide information about, or a way of working with, a core theme around which future beliefs about the self might gather. Understanding this process may result in resolving some issues and provide valuable information about the way we experience other transitions in our life.

This appears to hold true whether or not the significance attributed to the birth story is real or imagined, the important factor being that significance was perceived.

Exercise – Compiling and Witnessing the Birth Story

Exploring this important area of self-understanding can be a powerful experience and it is strongly recommended that you have a counsellor or therapist to help and support you. A trusted close friend can bear witness if you don't initially want to go to a counsellor. The easiest way to begin is to write down what you know, sense and think about your birth story in as much detail as you can. It may consist of factual information such as time and place, anecdotal parts that you've heard and believed over the years, your own inner belief and feelings about your birth, impressions, images, and dreams. If images come into your mind as you write, make a note of them, sketch them (don't worry if you can't draw, just make a rough outline to remind yourself). This is your story, and though it necessarily consists of some information given by others, you will find as you work, you have your own sense of events too.

Another area to note down; many families have sayings about the children and their births. One mother always used to say about her daughter's breach birth, "she came out backwards and has been going through life backwards ever since". A father used to say with exasperation about his teenage son, "he kept us waiting when he was being born, he still keeps us waiting at every opportunity." These sayings, usually said in a jokey way, form part of the family myth and are important in understanding what you believe about yourself. Take a moment to think of the implications of such statements, what it would mean if they were constantly repeated to a child. Are there any sayings in your own family about you and your birth?

Once you have compiled your story in as much detail as you feel necessary, you need your witness and sufficient space and time free of interruption. Witnessing the telling of your story is an

31

important role, you need someone you can trust and feel comfortable with. Reading out your story is the first step. Ask your witness not to interrupt with questions, but to listen supportively and attentively. After the first reading, see how you feel. You might want to go through the story again, thinking what different parts mean. You might want your witness at some point to feedback to you their understanding of what you've said, while bearing in mind that it is your own interpretation that is important. It may take more than one session of witnessing to feel you have explored this. For some people, witnessing is enough. Others might want to go further and explore areas, perhaps with a counsellor, to gain understanding of this important first transition.

Chapter 4
Personality and Interactions

As the personality forms around the emerging soul, we have seen that the mother (or the primary carer) in particular is responsible for boundaries, for keeping the child safe, in the early years. The father helps with this, and with back-up at all levels. In an ideal world, this would be enough. But we are not perfect beings living in a perfect world and inevitably things happen to and around the child that leave their mark.

Layers of growth in the personality can be imagined as the rings of a growing tree. If you look at a mature tree you can see how events such as unseasonable weather have affected its growth; drought causing less growth, wet seasons causing a growth spurt. Diseases can cause the tree to grow bark over and around an impediment, leaving a bulge or lesion. Foreign bodies can affect growth; a tie used to secure a sapling to a stake becomes embedded in the substance of the tree, and the tree thickens and grows round it.

In Diagram 4 we see areas of personality that have been affected in some way at different ages. Small inclusions or scar tissue form and affect how the personality functions, to a greater or lesser degree depending on the severity of the original impact and the individual's response to it. Imagine, for example, a humiliating experience at school, perhaps witnessed by peers. If the individual responds naturally at the time, the impact and the experience is digested and integrated in the personality. In other words, we have considered what has happened, learnt from it and absorbed the experience.

Layers of growth in the personality

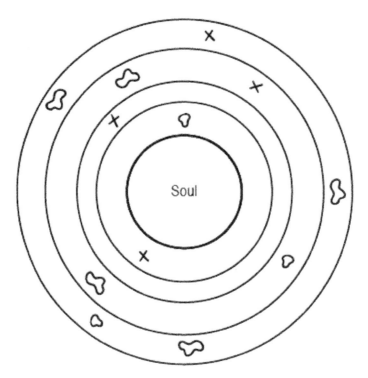

✕ ◌ ᑕᑐ - Undigested and unintegrated experiences

Diag. 4

If the individual is unable to respond naturally and is wounded by the experience, it can leave a mark. A defensive layer, which can be likened to scar tissue forms around the impact, isolating it and protecting the personality from its effects. It is not resolved and integrated into the personality. Most experiences thus protected will be remembered but the personality is protected to some extent from re-experiencing the depth of original pain.

Some experiences are so painful that protection may be correspondingly greater, resulting in the event being 'forgotten' or repressed from conscious memory. Even if the original incident is not remembered, it can be triggered by circumstances with like energy. Feelings similar to those experienced in the original incident are triggered at a level deeper than memory. They may not stop the person doing what he or she wants to in life, but they may inhibit and bring feelings of discomfort or fear. To refer to our simple example, appearing in front of a group of peers can bring repeated fears of humiliation, maybe not fully understood at a conscious level.

There are many ways for scar tissue to form. Experiences of being prematurely torn away from parents, perhaps a baby taken into hospital away from familiar surroundings and safe boundaries, will be registered in this way. Abusive relationships leave a mark, times when a person may feel in danger of losing their life, being pushed into the next step too soon by ambitious or even by neglectful parents as well as many everyday occurrences which have affected how vulnerable we feel.

Every personality responds uniquely. For example, siblings will often recount the same childhood incident quite differently. Much depends on the inherent traits, on the essence of the being, on the child's position in the family and on subtle differences in the way parents treat children. These are all normal and natural occurrences and responses, and do not indicate mental instability or abnormality.

Generally, for most of us, the personality boundary retains a certain permeability, giving an element of choice. Exchanges of an emotional, intimate and even soul nature are possible. Such exchanges are indicated in Diagram 5 by arrows.

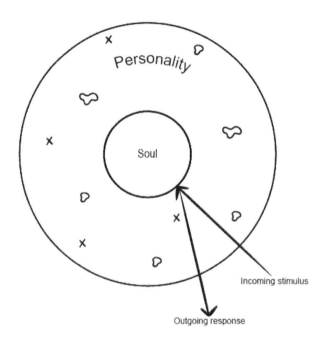

Diag 5
Interactions – Soul to Soul

Falling in love can be an experience which reaches the soul. The feeling of being completely open to another human being is a powerful one, and we can see that this will be a vulnerable time, bypassing all we have learned instinctively about psychological safety and all the warnings in our psyche about being alert to potential hurts.

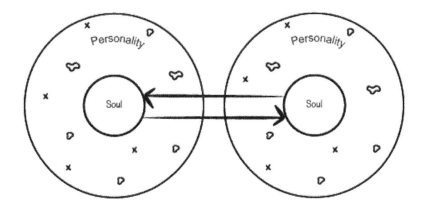

Diag. 5-a
soul to soul intimate exchange

It may also be a time of strength, when we feel we can conquer the world and love everyone, even our enemies. This is the nature of the soul, at once vulnerable on the earth plane while bringing strength and love beyond our imaginings.

When a love affair starts to break up, the pain seems intolerable. We wonder if we will survive. Our deepest levels are wounded and another scar or defensive layer is added.

Each mark on the tree-ring diagram represents an occurrence when we were hurt, some small and minor, some deeper and more lasting in effect. For most of us, there is plenty of our personality left unscarred. Combining Diagrams 4, 5 and 6 illustrates how we interact once our personality has developed scars. Scar tissue protects the vulnerable mind and soul from the effects of the unintegrated experience. An experience or interaction is blocked by the scar tissue which in effect means we respond from that defence, not the real place of soul.

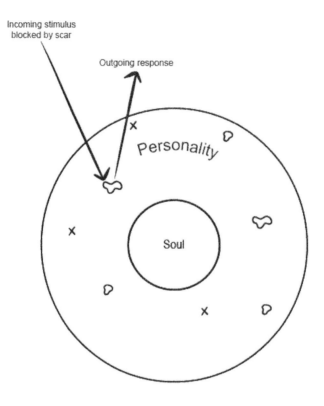

Diag. 6
Interactions – some blocked

But as we saw in Diagram 5, interactions can avoid the scars and still reach our open soul level. We may not only survive broken relationships but live to fall in love again. However, we may be wary or sceptical, fearful of being hurt because of past experiences. Any experience which has a similar feel to another in the past, contains within it the potential to trigger the original wounding. Such exchanges may 'bounce off' the scar and never reach the soul. The potential for these interactions is reduced because they are restricted by scar tissue which has formed as protection in response to the original incident.

The personality's job is to allow expression of and to protect the soul. An adequate response may come from the unintegrated material, but the response will not have the same depth.

It is important to state again that this may not be a conscious process. We are not constantly thinking 'I'm afraid because ten years ago such and such happened'. We just know we experience difficulties in this particular situation today. When levels of fear inhibit how one copes with life, it is possible to seek help from a psychotherapist or counsellor whose role in this instance is to help the individual integrate past issues or traumas.

It is also important to state the obvious; an individual does not have to learn to express him or herself. It is a natural impulse. If expression is inhibited in some way, it is because that has been learnt through painful experience.

More rarely, an individual becomes so traumatised that the layers of scar tissue completely circle the soul. This person may apparently function well on a surface level, or there may be some noticeable personality disorder. Either way, the soul is so well protected from further trauma that all exchanges of an emotional, intimate or soul nature are blocked. Recovery is still possible with the help of a suitably trained therapist and the individual's own dedication to the process.

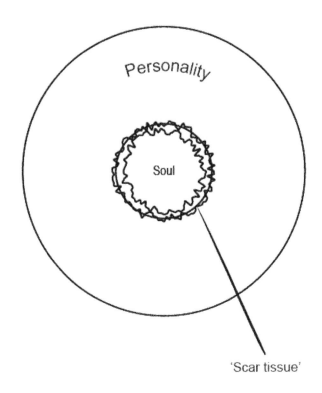

'Scar tissue'

Diag. 7
scarring round soul

The earth plane is the only plane of existence where we encounter other individuals in this way, where we clash and hurt each other, hide our true nature, and generally protection and defence are necessary parts of life and experience on this plane.

I should re-affirm here that the soul remains unaffected by the events of the personality or personality behaviour patterns, in so far as it remains whole.

It has been said too many times that hurts and traumas all represent opportunities for growth, even that we should be grateful to those who hurt us for giving us the chance to move on. Too easily the vulnerable and wounded individual feels even more helpless, despairing, worthless or angry in the face of such statements. The personality comes with emotions of all kinds, not just love and joy but also anger and bitterness. This is what it is to be human, a soul clothed in a physical body in order to experience life on the earth plane. If we so choose, and find the opportunity, we can work through the hurt and pain and come out the other side feeling calmer, at peace with ourselves. There is no 'should' about it; we have a choice even when it seems that we are buffeted by our raging feelings. As we learn to be at peace with ourselves, we find that bitterness and anger fall away and we begin to accept other people as well as ourselves in all our joint humanity.

Chapter 5
Introduction to the Chakras

Mind, Body and Spirit are words which are bandied about in many self-help books, and indeed they form an essential trinity we need to live and operate on the earth plane. Physical attributes and actions are influenced by the mind or emotional state of the individual, consciously or unconsciously. Much has been written about behavioural psychology, psychosomatic issues etc should you wish to follow up this aspect. It is not my intention to do more than include it as a vital component in the way we live.

Mind and Spirit are, in such usage, the shorthand words covering Emotional/Psychological and Spiritual journeying. We are seeing how they are inextricably linked in the way we function, and we have seen how the incoming soul needs protection against heavy earth energies, protection partly provided by the personality. But we are fundamentally spiritual beings incarnate in physical bodies, and as such retain the ability to function as spiritual beings, albeit in a more limited fashion than on the soul plane. A system which plays an important part in our ability to do this is called the chakra system.

The energy field that surrounds and interpenetrates the body is now measurable and can be photographed by a process called Kirlian photography. It may be referred to as the aura or personal energy field. There are several layers to this field and within it, chakras are points or centres of energy.

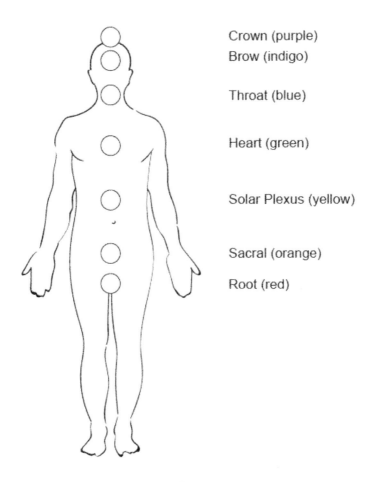

Crown (purple)
Brow (indigo)

Throat (blue)

Heart (green)

Solar Plexus (yellow)

Sacral (orange)

Root (red)

Diag. 8
Chakra System

Seven major chakras form a network relating to different parts of the physical body. There are other chakras but the seven included in the next chapter cover everyday physiological, psychological and some spiritual living. The seven work as a team and often their references overlap.

Each chakra is responsible for maintaining a different colour in the aura.

To a Sensitive (i.e. a person able to see beyond the immediate physical plane) the aura appears as an ovoid of light surrounding the body, with swirling colours. The distance it extends from the body varies, according to health and circumstances.

A chakra appears to a Sensitive as a vortex of light within the aura. It appears as a spiral, a shape regarded as a kind of blueprint throughout the natural world. You might start to visualise a chakra by thinking of a rose, a spiral shell, a whirlpool, all displaying the same kind of spiral form within a circle.

Each chakra appears to rotate at a different rate, the lower chakras of the body rotating more slowly than those placed higher in the body. Lower and higher are not used here as evaluatory terms but denote the vertical position in the human body.

As well as the personal energy field, there is energy all around us, in trees and plants, in the earth and sea, in the atmosphere of places eg churches and other holy or quiet sites. It is available for our use, and collectively these other fields may be referred to as the universal energy field. In order to make use of it, we need to find a part of ourselves which can tolerate or work with the same vibration. Chakras form these access points, vibrating at different rates as their rotation speeds vary. They have the ability to convert energy to a vibration suitable for our use; an analogy might be an electrical transformer. The whole system operates in a way similar to the physical nervous system. We are unaware of its action, unless we start to study it. We may also become aware if something goes wrong, disease etc.

The whirling of energy creates a vortex with a central space or core which attracts other energy down into it. Each chakra therefore is capable of receiving energy from external sources, and also from other people. Our perception of other people is partly based on what we receive at this level, and may be called 'gut feeling'. It is unconscious or intuitive until we start to work with the chakras.

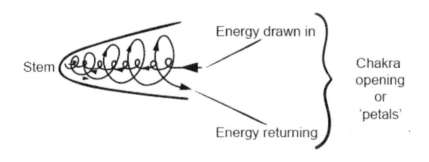

Diag. 9
Chakra energy

Energy pours into the chakra via the central core and then spirals out again along the edges of the cone-shaped chakra, dispersing in the auric field or back into the universal field. Compare inhaling air followed by exhalation back into the surrounding air. As with breath entering the lungs to exchange gases, we have the opportunity to take something we need from the energy entering the chakra before it spirals back out.

In this way, chakras distribute energy throughout our system, allowing it to flow from one level to another. To go back to one of the natural spiral analogies, picture a whirlpool. The pattern it makes is both *in* and *of* the water, carrying things supported in it from one level to another. Our individual energy field interpenetrates the physical body, i.e. it exists both within the body and outside of it, and so too do the chakras. They extend out into the auric space, the egg-shaped individual energy field.

In the course of life, chakras may become overcharged with too much energy, or depleted with too little. Blockages may also occur, in much the same way as in the formation of the personality. These inhibit the function of the chakras. The chakras therefore are indicators of well-being and dis-ease, both physical and psychological, with patterns of ill health often showing in the chakras before they manifest at a physical level. Areas of particular skill will also show in the distinctive energy of a chakra eg. a singer or orator may have a large, bright or energetic throat chakra.

Chakras may be brought back into balance or blockages released by some forms of healing which work on the subtle as well as physical levels, eg. homeopathy, acupuncture, Bach Flower Remedies, forms of energy healing such as Reiki and spiritual healing. Self healing in the form of visualisation and breathing techniques also help to keep the chakras balanced and healthy, offering the optimum level of well-being for the individual. See the end of this chapter for suggested exercise.

The chakra system begins to form while the soul nears the foetus, along with the development of other nervous systems. When a baby is born, the chakras are reported by Sensitives to be pink, but as development continues, each chakra takes on a characteristic colour. In the early stages the chakras are

46

extremely sensitive, and unconsciously and automatically the parents' energy systems will protect the child from too much intrusion at this delicate stage.

During physical and emotional development and during the formation and strengthening of the personality, the chakra system grows too, building a complete subtle framework. The chakras record and contain the patterns of our development. Everything we have talked about which goes into our make-up is stored or reflected in the appropriate chakra, the physiological, psychological and spiritual make-up of the individual. As well as the essence brought into incarnation by the soul, influences will have been felt from parents, from the kind of society and culture we are born into, and as we progress, from habits we ourselves create, from the influence of our peers, and from experiences we have had. The energy pattern of each chakra is therefore unique to the individual.

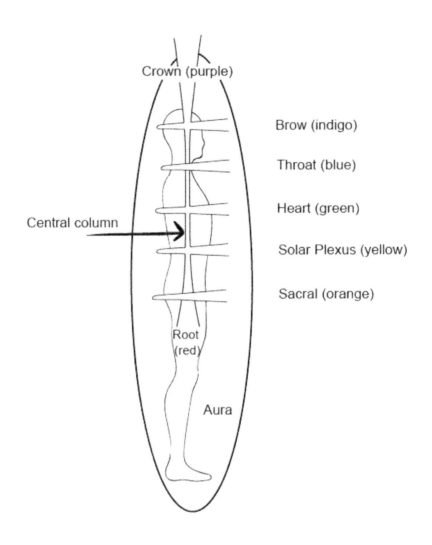

Crown (purple)

Brow (indigo)

Throat (blue)

Heart (green)

Central column

Solar Plexus (yellow)

Sacral (orange)

Root (red)

Aura

Diag. 10

Position of the chakras
side view showing cone shaped chakras
interpenetrating physical body and extending into aura.

The chakras or energy centres in the subtle energy system all feed into a central column, located close to the physical spinal column. Energy flows along the central column in both directions, linking all the chakras. It also forms a link with the energy of the earth through the root, and with spiritual energy through the crown. Just as with the chakras, blockages can occur here and can be cleared by visualisation and breathing, or by one of the healing methods already mentioned. See the end of this chapter for suggested exercise.

Just as you shower, clean your teeth etc for your physical well-being, it is wise as you continue with your evolving awareness and development to have a daily or regular spiritual routine. This should be tailored to your individual needs and can include any of the exercises mentioned in this book, whichever you find helpful. Set aside a time and a space, however small, where you can practice these quietly and undisturbed. It might feel right to have nearby a candle, or crystals, or other objects meaningful to you.

Exercises in clearing the chakras and the central column follow.

Exercise clearing individual chakras

For all these exercises, you need to have familiarised yourself with the position of each chakra. Sit or lie down comfortably, without crossing arms or legs, (lotus position is ok) in a quiet place where you are unlikely to be disturbed, remembering to turn off your phone.
Begin to breathe slowly and rhythmically, and try to become aware of the rhythm.
When you feel ready, move your awareness with your breath to a chakra you wish to cleanse, and continue breathing in through the front of the chakra or 'petals', and back out. See Diagram 9. After a while, you may start to become aware of the colours or energy of the chakra. Hold in mind that breathing in takes in healing and/or cleansing energy, while breathing out releases negativity or anything that may cause the chakra not to function at its best.

On finishing, gently visualise the closing of the petals, not tightly, just gently. Visualise a blessing in the form of a cross of white light surrounded by a circle of light, or a star of light in a circle of light. The cross if used, should be equal length arms.

Slowly become aware of your surroundings, and stretch. Ten minutes is a good time for this exercise till you are accustomed to it.

Work with each chakra in turn, starting with the root chakra, remembering its orientation within the body.

Exercise clearing the central column

You can keep the central column clear in the same way as the chakras. Same sitting position and conditions for all these visualisations.

When the rhythm of your breath is established, let your awareness enter through the Root chakra, continuing up the central column. You can change to the out breath around the heart centre and continue up and out through the Crown. Breathe in and start back down the central column, through the Crown, changing to the out breath around the area of the heart chakra, and out through the Root.

These two exercises done regularly will help maintain health, breathing in cleansing energy and breathing out anything not needed. After a while you may become aware of not just colours but sensations and energies, maybe becoming aware of any blockages or hinderances as you breathe. If you encounter this, just gently breathe through it, no need to force it. You will start to appreciate what feels right for you and what you need to let go.

Chapter 6
The Chakras

See Appendix 3 for table of easy reference.

This chapter will give an overview of individual chakras. For simplification, keywords are given but it is highly recommended that to understand the importance of the chakras in physiological, psychological and spiritual well-being, a reliable book should be studied. See Appendix 2 for suggestions.

Each chakra contains all colours, but each is particularly attuned to one colour. It is responsible for this colour in the subtle energy field of the aura, sometimes over-producing when the chakra is highly charged, sometimes under-producing when the chakra is depleted for some reason such as illness or over-use. This is the mundane colour, evident in everyday activities. Other colours are associated with each chakra, evident during activities such as meditation, healing, praying, work which responds to the needs of others which may be called service, and so on.

Bear in mind that each stage linked with a chakra is not necessarily confined to the associated developmental age. These are offered as a guideline, while in reality, the stages are often more fluid, with overlap and revisiting highly possible.

Root Chakra

The root chakra is located at the perineum, midway between the anus and the genitals. Unlike most of the other chakras which have a horizontal orientation, the root faces down between the legs, with the stem going up into the central column. Vertical orientation. Look back at Diagram 10 to get a visual sense of this if it isn't familiar to you.

The predominant colour of the root is red, a strong colour which grounds us in the earth. Other colours associated with the root are brown and mauve, colours which while still relating to the earth have an added dimension.

The sense of smell is connected to the root chakra, the first sense a baby develops outside the womb. A sense with powerful instinctive use, we 'smell' danger, fear and sexual readiness, often at a level below conscious awareness. Subliminally, the information we gather through our sense of smell adds to a store we use to determine actions at an instinctive level, such as the 'fight or flight' mechanism.

The developmental stage is linked to birth and the years the child is discovering himself as a separate individual, apart from his mother. Boundaries are much needed. Age 0 – 3 years.

The building blocks of the human body are related to the root chakra: the skin, bones, muscles and tendons. Diseases involving these may be helped by working with this chakra. Other areas linked to this chakra are the testes and ovaries as part of our instinct and drive towards survival.

Ways of nurturing this chakra are earth-related: gardening or any contact with the earth such as walking in the countryside, barefoot when possible, the smell of earth, the sight and touch of trees. Twigs, pebbles or other natural materials used in the home act as grounding agents and reminders. The chakra can also respond to colour used in clothing or decorating your living space, or simply having an item in your work space to remind you. If you feel too energised in this area, overly defensive or too 'down to earth', you may have too much red; try introducing browns and mauves into your personal space for balance. All of these activities need to be done consciously to obtain the most benefit.

The root chakra represents our connection with earth and is a vital channel for bringing in more earth-energy as well as for discharging stress or anything we do not need. It is a two-way dynamic process.

Keywords are Rootedness (connection to earth), Instinct (particularly about survival), Physical Energy and the Physical Body.

Sacral

The sacral chakra is located two fingers below the navel and has a horizontal orientation, going through front to back, to the sacrum area of the spine.

The predominant colour of the sacral is orange, a bold warm colour of raw emotional energy. Other colours associated with this chakra are amber and gold, higher vibrations of orange.

The parts of the body connected to the sacral chakra are concerned with fluids; arteries and veins, the lymph system and blood, the processes by which the body is nurtured and internally cleansed, eliminating unwanted material.

The sense of taste is linked to the sacral. This is the sensation of enjoying food as well as aesthetic taste.

The sacral chakra's developmental stage is linked to the child becoming an individual in his own right, finding out what his own tastes might be in every way. The child still needs guidance and some (but less) help with boundaries, and is on a path of discovery outside his own immediate self. This can be a very creative time for many children. There is often the discovery that what has been taken for granted eg. food can also be a source of pleasure, and pleasure too begins to manifest in enjoying the company of the other sex, a move away from the instinctive level of the root chakra and the beginning of an appreciation of the differences in gender. Often during this phase, a sibling is born into the family, bringing twin issues of rivalry and companionship. The sense of others increases. Age 3 – 8 years approximately.

Water has long been used as a symbol for emotions, and in the sacral we find a watery theme running through. Therefore, ways of nurturing this chakra include being by the sea or large bodies of water, experiencing the energy of such areas. Running water, waterfalls and rivers can be helpful too. Even showering with conscious intent can be beneficial on more than just the physical level. Using the chakra's colour with caution is also helpful. Bright orange can be too much, too bold, either in the home or in dress, but shades of amber and gold can be introduced with a calming effect on the sacral. Food such as oranges or their juice are beneficial. All of these activities need to be done consciously to obtain the most benefit.

Keywords for the sacral chakra are Emotional Energy, a Sense of Others, Creativity.

Solar Plexus Chakra

The solar plexus chakra is located between the lower end of the sternum and the navel, with a horizontal orientation, the stem going through to the back.

The predominant colour of the solar plexus is yellow, a pure clean colour not without warmth. Other colours associated with this chakra are gold and rose. If you watch a sunset or sunrise, you will see that gold and rose are linked as one fades imperceptibly into the other.

The sense of sight is associated with the solar plexus; physical sight, the ability to envisage creative ideas you want to bring to fruition, and vision of a fore-seeing nature or psychic intuition. Those who attempt to give psychic readings using only this chakra are unreliable. The wisdom of the heart and the self-responsibility of the throat chakras are needed before we reach the psychic or spiritual insight of the brow chakra.

The solar plexus chakra's developmental stage is linked to the time when a child starts to think for himself, to formulate his own ideas from the questions and discoveries he has been making up to now. His sense of reason is developing. He is moving away from needing parental boundaries, getting ready to make his own and rebel against those he finds restrictive. No longer reliant on others to make things happen, he initiates things for himself. A sense of power comes with this, which can be both exhilarating and fearful. There is a fiery-ness about this initiatory stage, and the element of fire is often linked with the solar plexus, particularly the sun's energy. Age 8 –12 years approximately.

The adrenal glands are connected to the solar plexus, the glands which supply adrenalin and energy for every situation. During prolonged stressful situations, production and reserves sometimes cannot meet the demand, and rest and recuperation are urgently required. Exhaustion or fatigue may indicate this state. When the chakra is working well, we feel energised and confident in our abilities.

Sun shining on the solar plexus itself is particularly energising, taking the usual precautions against over-exposure, but walking in sunshine, seeing the rays shine down through a break in the clouds or dappling the ground beneath trees are also very helpful. In winter, sitting in front of a log fire, watching with conscious intent the intense yellow-gold in the flames, brings similar but fewer benefits by remind us. When particular clarity of vision is needed, perhaps during a period of intense study, having pure yellow around is helpful, eg. a silk scarf, something appropriate in out workspace. Rose is the colour used to calm, and especially in conjunction with nourishing gold for recovery during periods of exhaustion. All of these activities need to be conscious to get the most benefit.

Keywords are Personal Power, Drive, Initiating, Reason.

Heart

The heart chakra is located at the level of the physical heart, but more central. It has a horizontal orientation, the stem going through to the back.

The predominant colour of the heart chakra is a fresh verdant green. Other associated colours are rose, and rose-amethyst, a pink that is going towards mauve.

The sense of touch is linked to the heart chakra. Physical touch is essential for children to feel loved and for them to thrive. But 'touch' can imply tenderness, being moved, being touched by love or concern for another.

The heart chakra's developmental stage is connected to the years of adolescence. The feeling quality here is different from the raw emotion of the sacral. We have become aware of others and their needs, and of the attraction and love we might feel for them. We feel touched by other people. Heart to heart, soul to soul communication and interaction is powerful and yet leaves us feeling vulnerable. Sacral love has an element of selfishness about it, loving because the person is beautiful or because they have something to offer us. The challenge of heart level love is to be compassionate and unconditional, to accept people as they are, not as we want them to be. This includes self-acceptance, seeing our own worth without justifying it by status, wealth, self-sacrifice. Young people feel tender and vulnerable while making this transition, and though they still need boundaries and guidelines, they also need increasing freedom to make their own choices and find their own limits. Age 12 –15 years.

In the heart chakra, we are beginning to move away from the mundane and more physical aspects. It offers a refinement of the qualities that have gone before in the root, sacral and solar plexus, and an indication of what is to come in the throat, brow and crown. The quality of emotion has changed from instinctive and raw, moving towards unconditional. Similarly, the way we understand the world is changing too. The heart chakra at its best provides a discerning, non-judgemental viewpoint, detachment without indifference. In loving, it is not possessive, it is the kind of love which allows air to flow between two people, giving each a space to develop while holding them unconditionally. The higher ideals of the upper chakras begin to be seen as a possibility.

It is not surprising that roses are often given as a gift of love; roses feed the heart with their scent, their shape and their rose-pink colours. Leaf green – the colour of new leaves in spring – heals and nourishes the heart. You might walk in a garden or woods or fields, taking in this colour. And walking on green hillsides where you feel the air flowing around you is very helpful in freeing up emotions and getting a sense of moving on towards the higher aspects of love.

The heart also needs to feel touch and to touch others. Physical therapies such as aromatherapy, using rose oil, soothe a sore heart. Allowing ourselves to feel and accept the compliments of friends and lovers has a beneficial effect, and although that sounds simplistic, think how often people – maybe each of us – deflect compliments. The heart itself begins to open and blossom during the process of helping others; if the urge is there to be of service, follow it, using your discernment as a check and balance. All of these activities need to be conscious to be beneficial.

Keywords are Love, Love of Others, Tenderness, Compassion, Non-judgementalism.

Throat

The throat chakra is located at the physical throat area in a horizontal orientation, the stem going through to the back of the neck.

The predominant colour of the throat is blue, a kind of vibrant cornflower blue. Other colours associated with the throat are silver and turquoise.

The sense of hearing is linked to this chakra which may sound surprising at first. It has a dual meaning; to hear and to be heard, and so the chakra is linked not only to hearing others, but also to how we make ourselves heard, how we speak and the quality of our voice, how we express ourselves.

The throat chakra is the last of the developmental chakras and so is a gateway chakra, forming the last of the series with the lower chakras and the first of a trinity with the higher chakras. In practical terms, it covers the age when an individual accepts responsibility for himself, perhaps leaving home, earning his own living. For others, there may be a period of intense study with all the pressures of exams and expectations. This period, for many cultures, covers the traditional 'coming of age', an initiation into the wider world which recognises individuality and self-responsibility. Parental boundaries are left behind. Age 15 – 21 years.

The way we speak has a direct bearing on how we are heard. Because the chakras operate as a team, unfinished learning or issues with the lower chakras will show up in the way we speak or the kind of language we use.

Examples might be:

If we have unresolved survival issues lodged in the root chakra, we may be very demanding of attention in the way we express ourselves, a sort of 'look at me' voice.

If we have nurturing issues connected to the sacral, neediness shows in our response to others.

If we have power and control issues connected to the solar plexus, we will show our defensiveness in conversation whenever we feel verbally threatened or confronted, either by backing off or by aggression.

If we speak with love in our voice we are more likely to evoke love. Similarly, if we hear love in the voice of another, we are more likely to respond in like manner. Much depends on how open the heart chakra is.

The energy of the throat is very creative; singing, acting, public speaking, telling stories. The whole range of the colour blue is beneficial to the throat chakra. Turquoise or aquamarine are especially good for strengthening the voice of those who speak to large numbers of people. You can consciously remind yourself of this by wearing a scarf of these colours, by wearing a pendant with turquoise or aquamarine gemstone, or carrying the gemstone with you. Silver heals the throat chakra. There is much to do to aid the expression of this chakra, depending on the individual. The sight and scent of a bluebell wood can open the chakra and help ease the transition into the upper chakra values. Having blue flowers around the house, some blue or silver in the soft furnishings, wearing blues and silver all have a beneficial and easing effect if you feel you have difficulty expressing yourself. Singing in the shower might be a fun side to healing the throat, bringing confidence in your own sound. There are sound therapists of various kinds, some who train the voice, others who work at an energy level and help the individual to release old blockages, heal old wounds in this chakra. All of these actions need to be done consciously to bring the most benefits.

Keywords are Communication, Self-Expression, Self-Responsibility.

Brow

The brow chakra is located between and slightly above the eyes, traditionally known as the third eye, with a horizontal orientation, the stem going through to the back of the head.

The predominant colour of the brow chakra is Indigo. Associated colours are turquoise and mauve.

In the higher chakras, we leave behind the senses associated with the physical body, the personality has matured though is always open to refinement. We are moving into higher vibrations of the brow and crown chakras, and therefore into more spiritual levels of perception. Sight is linked with the brow, but not physical sight as with the solar plexus. The brow is connected with spiritual vision, with beginning to see the progress and development of the self in a clearer way, with using intuition and insight. Having lived through the developmental years, the individual can look back and begin to make sense of his physical and emotional progress. Without some psychological understanding of the personality and its quirks, true spiritual progress is often more difficult. Leaving behind the demands of the personality is more safely done by gaining understanding of the journey made by the personality. The brow chakra helps with the integration of this understanding, leading on to the realisation of the spiritual beings we are.

Usually, the indications that we are moving into a more spiritually aware period of our lives are in small glimpses of clarity, joy, centredness and unity with all beings. These fleeting moments build until we begin to access these states with more consciousness. For a few people, this awareness is precipitated by a crisis, an accident or illness. But generally, steady progress

64

is brought about by application to the way we have chosen.

Many of us avoid the responsibilities of moving forward on our spiritual path – even though it may be much desired – by busyness, leaving less room for the glimpses which would encourage and carry us forward.

We can encourage the brow chakra to open and work for us by meditation, by making sure there are periods of silence and stillness in our lives, by appreciation of beauty leading to the qualities of mystery, wonder, awe and compassion. A sense of timelessness and an aura of peace characterise spiritual experience and qualities.

Working and living with colours can heal blockages and let the brow energy begin to flow.

Alongside personal integration, the brow is connected with higher and broader thought, inspiration and intuition, with philosophy and world view, with belief systems. Using this centre, our perception can shift up a gear. Negative expression would be living too much in the imagination, or too much in the past if there are unresolved issues clouding clear use of the brow energy. Positive imagination, visualisation of our aspirations and appreciation of other people and aspiring to help them, uses brow energy as its best. As with the other chakras, conscious awareness of these things aids growth.

Keywords for the brow chakra are Imagination, Inspiration, Insight, Self-realisation.

Crown

The crown chakra is located at the top of the head and, like the root, has a different orientation to other chakras. It has a vertical orientation with the stem going down into the central column. Diagram 10.

The predominant colour of the crown is purple-violet with white and gold offering extra dimensions. Violet is a cleansing colour; eg: ultra violet light is used as a water purifying treatment to destroy bacteria. White has connotations of purity; in some traditions white is the colour of the robes worn by acolytes entering Orders as if they were children, innocence renewed as they renounce the world. Gold is the supreme colour, with links to the Sun, the ultimate power without which we could not exist in our world. Symbolism of gold is a subject in itself, often representing God, holiness, power.

The crown is part of the whole team of chakras, but also has a role as part of the trinity (with throat and brow) which forms a connection to and allows expression of soul consciousness. As with the throat and brow, any unresolved issues or blockages in the lower chakras will also affect the flow of energy in the crown. An individual with a clear well-functioning crown chakra will have a whole vision of life with few prejudices, dependencies or attachments. We are able to come into a sense of our own power and to use it wisely and responsibly.

We become aware that knowledge is not enough for its own sake, it has to be grounded (root), assimilated and digested (sacral), tempered with logic and reason (solar plexus), burnished with love and discernment (heart), used creatively (throat) and with intuition (brow). Knowledge is not a finite or static part of our consciousness but is a constantly shifting and changing aspect of it. Balanced by steady progress and self-development, knowledge becomes wisdom, greater than the sum of individual pieces of information. As our soul consciousness increases, we are able to use all that we may be to the optimum level.

Necessarily, in talking about the crown chakra and soul consciousness, we are delving into metaphysical areas. A summary of all that has gone before will suffice to bring us up to this level for the purpose of this book. Psychologically we need a personality to give us drive and energy to exist on this plane, to transform energies which would be too dense, too heavy, for the incoming soul to deal with. We need it in order to relate to others, and when we are hurting in relationship, we need it to provide us with defences to prevent us being overwhelmed by emotional pain. Given these reasons for the existence of the personality (some would say ego), it would be unwise to try to transcend or let go the personality, leaving us unprotected, without doing all the work required to reach such a point.

To expand a little. In the 1960's and 1970's, the Western world experienced an influx of Eastern philosophies and religion, leading in some cases to misinterpretation of this part of the process. Without the long, hard – and joyful – process of psychological understanding and development of a healthy personality alongside our chosen spiritual practice, we should not try to surrender our personality needs or personal responsibility.

Surrender at the crown chakra is about letting go the attachments we have made in the past, letting them go because we have outgrown the need for them. Maybe we have become attached to making more money than we really need, or to eating far more food than we require for health, for example.

67

Surrender is about a constant re-assessment of our lives to see what we can let go step by step. It is not a single event. It is a process of refining. Then we might say we have surrendered to the process of becoming who we can truly be. In this instance, surrender has connotations of release and trust.

Keywords for the crown chakra are Knowledge, Surrender, Soul Consciousness.

Chapter 7
Difficulties in Practice

Single and absent parents, transitions.

In looking at a cycle, one complete incarnation, birth is the first transition, providing the background for all future transitions in the life. Our views on appropriate birthing change over time. With the emphasis on antisepsis, birth in hospital became the favoured method, rather than only for emergencies, and more babies and mothers survived. But our understanding of hygiene allowed more women to give birth in their own homes, and natural childbirth again became the vogue. Now we have a mixture of hospital births, with Caesarian sections etc on offer, and home births with modern methods of preparation and birthing. What does all this mean for the incoming soul?

In preparing for incarnation, conditions are studied, and choices made to give the incoming soul the best possible chance of appropriate development. The soul indicates a willingness to undergo incarnation and undertake further learning. This might include the willingness to parent a child. During our earth incarnation, this information is not available to us, and so women who have not thought of giving birth may find themselves pregnant 'accidentally' or by means outside their conscious control. The soul has indicated willingness to birth and parent; the personality is perhaps taken by surprise, or at least feels unprepared.

The soul's willingness provides, when the time comes, the subtle structure needed for holding the foetus, for helping to form the chakras and auras, processes which are unconscious to the personality.

In an ideal scenario, two parents share the task of providing the etheric mesh to hold the incoming soul until it reaches its birth hour. A couple deciding to have a child automatically begin preparations on the etheric level. It is more difficult to imagine what happens when the pregnancy is the result of a one-night stand, or rape. In some cases, and depending on his soul's wishes, the father may still provide etheric material, though at the personality level he may be totally unaware of the pregnancy. Or the work can fall to the single mother with help from a discarnate soul, that is a soul not choosing incarnation at that time but who is willing to take on a share in the birth process by giving energy and support from the spiritual plane. The single mother will often have the second layer of support around her supplied by a close friend or her own parents, or in some cases a care worker.

Let me say here that it is necessary, or at the very least desirable, for both male and female energies to contribute to this process. This may sound controversial in today's world, but those energies do not necessarily have to come from one male and one female. All of us have both masculine and feminine attributes; different types of activity and ways of being have been stereotyped so that we think of them as masculine or feminine, and indeed certain activities do require more of one energy than the other. To simplify down to the essence, masculine energy initiates and is outgoing, feminine energy is receptive and more inwardly tuned. But a woman may do the kind of work that requires initiatory action and so she uses the masculine energy within her. Jung called this animus. Similarly, a man may work in a traditional receptive feminine role, for example a therapist or nurse, using his feminine energy. Jung called this anima. Neither role precludes using other energies in appropriate ways, nor does it necessarily reflect sexual orientation. We are all a blend of what we call masculine and feminine; in some people, one is more dominant than the other, regardless of physical gender. In most people the appropriate energy is used naturally, depending on the task. Becoming aware of this process can enhance options and abilities.

Following this through, a female friend or the pregnant woman's own mother can provide the masculine energy to help set up the right conditions for the baby, on the unconscious level. Or they can use a mixture of each energy from each of the two women.

The birth process can be seen as a most crucial time, leaving behind the familiar unity of the soul plane where the soul has been at one with other beings, healed and cared for, to make the difficult transition to a physical body; the gradual falling away of awareness of unity and taking on the rigours of birth onto the earth plane, the sudden thrust into this world, the beginnings of personality. At the same time, the subtle systems of chakras and aura are building under the unconscious guidance of the mother, whose own energy system provides protection. If she has a loving partner, the mother and foetus have a second layer of protection around them.

Birth is a tough process for both mother and child. We have medical aids that ease pain, but much can be done to improve the surrounding conditions. The soul has rested in the etheric mesh, the physical foetus has floated in the amniotic fluid cushioned by softness and gentleness. Their coming together is a shock to the soul, which may be likened to putting on a cold wet constricting garment. Newly joined, the soul/foetus battles the way out into the earth plane to be greeted by bright white lights, metallic noises, relatively cool temperature, physically severed from all that has nurtured them. In some hospitals the baby is still taken away from the mother to a nursery. So many shocks, often traumas, to the newly developing systems.

Birth can be managed in a much more hospitable environment without compromising the hygienic qualities that ensure survival of mother and child. Women have instinctive knowledge of what is right for birth. Giving birth is one of the moments in life when a woman has closer access to the spirit world, to the intuitive pool of female wisdom. Knowing she is in control of the conditions which are right for her baby will bring her confidence and increase the sureness of her touch as a parent. For example, if she needs to walk, let her walk, if she needs to crouch, have a place where she can crouch. Laying flat on her back is not the most comfortable position in which to give birth for most women. Lower the lighting as far as possible, play soft music that the mother relates to.

Her partner or helper often assists her at the birth; providing strength and encouragement, calm and love will naturally widen his/her own aura to surround mother and child. If both parents follow their instincts, while maintaining rationality about safety for the birth, the subtle fields and energies follow automatically.

There are many theories about colours surrounding new babies. The colours of the chakras are still forming, new chakras being mostly pink before they take on their characteristic colours. Surrounding a baby with primary colours might be said to encourage the chakras to form, using these examples. But if we are thinking of the newly emerged soul, primary colours might be said to bombard him or her with too strong stimulus. Pastel colours – no matter whether pink or blue or other – may be gentler and more easily tolerated by the newborn of either sex.

All outside stimulus should be thought of in this way. The baby has been cocooned within the mother; noises, lights and smells diluted or non-existent until he is suddenly catapulted out into this harsh world. No one would think of giving a newborn baby highly spiced food instantly; milk and eventually thin cereal helps the developing digestive system. Loud noises and flashing or bright lights are the equivalent bombardment of the other senses. Soft music, soft lighting, pastel colours all provide a feeling of security and ease.

Often a young baby is taken into the parents' bed, or sleeps in the parents room. The chakras are open and attuned particularly to the parents. If the couple have sex in the child's presence, the chakras of the child will be bombarded by incomprehensible stimulus.

It has been said that generally we don't cope as well as we used to, that people in the past had no need of counselling for example, and that everyone lived closer together. Parents and children habitually slept in the same room and children learnt early about the sexual act. The inference is that we have become precious.

The fact is that we are developing souls who have reached a stage when development is speeding up. Generally speaking, we are becoming more sensitively attuned to spirit than we were. In the past we have been attuned more to the earth, to the seasons, to surviving. In our present era, our development is such that our subtle systems are more open to abuse and we are having to learn how to protect ourselves and how to be spiritual beings in physical bodies. Our children's chakras are more sensitive from the beginning. Part of our responsibilities as parents is to protect our young children from extreme influences. This is particularly true of a parent who might have different partners coming into the home, partners whose subtle energies are not attuned to the child. Time is needed to allow the child to become accustomed to the new energies.

Single parents of either sex have a tough time, trying to be all things to their child or children. Certainly, they have the energies within them to provide both the masculine and feminine qualities a child needs. But it is at a cost. Single parents are already stretched on a physical level, trying to earn sufficient money to raise their family, being the only person in the house to do all the chores, provide all the support, discipline etc that the child needs. Emotionally and spiritually, the single parent has a huge task, providing the subtle structures to safeguard the developing child, to provide the boundaries and guidance as the child grows and questions, and being the source of constant love and reassurance the child needs.

It is essential that single parents have support and help in their difficult and important parenting work. Single parents can help each other, forming formal groups or getting together simply as friends and neighbours. It spreads the load a little, but help from a source not already overstretched would work better.

Sometimes a single parent can turn to her own parents for help. The role of grandparents has been diminished as communities have drifted apart, sons and daughters relocated many miles away. And since the 1960's we have had a growing youth culture, reducing the respect or acknowledgement given to older people. But as society changes and the numbers of single parents increase, or both parents have to work, grandparents can and do play an important part in providing levels of emotional and subtle support.

Not everyone experiences ideal conditions of conception, pregnancy, birth and child rearing. It is important to do one's best within the circumstances, and it's also important not to get hung up about being a perfect parent. That sets up a too high expectation, followed by guilt that we don't achieve the impossible ideal, leaving us frustrated or worse, despairing. Not good for the child or parent. Research shows that as long as we are 'good enough' parents, the child will thrive. Remember that phrase – 'good enough' – it is important in so many endeavours. No one has to be perfect.

So we are seeing how important birth is as the first transition of this incarnation, how we might improve things for our incoming child with just a little awareness and intuition. Many first-time parents are nervous and afraid or reluctant to ask for what they need, what their instincts tell them is right for them as a new family being formed in our world. As long as the birth is safeguarded, is hygienic and safe, the parents could be allowed a lot of leeway in their choices, a process I believe is in progress right now.

Chapter 8
Boundaries and Protection
Intimacy, Personal space, and psychic protection.

Incarnation on the earth plane is full of opportunities, learning to be 'human and physical' while acknowledging our spiritual essence. This plane is where we learn about separateness and where we may clash with others, in a way that doesn't happen on spiritual planes of existence. Relationships, with all their difficulties, pain and joys, offer one of the greatest paths to growth, one reason why this text focuses on the way we communicate.

On the soul plane we interact with other souls in ways we can barely imagine from our earthly perspective. A sense of unity and lack of ego, the harmony and trust implied in that, are the norm. In incarnation we depend on our ego-personality for protection and as a way of relating to and communicating with other people.

The incoming soul leaves behind the plane of union but for several months is in a state of union with the mother. We come to incarnation knowing how to be at one and we experience it in the womb. Ideally, birth will be followed by bonding with the parents, separation from them at an appropriate time and becoming an individual. There are other scenarios which might follow.

For some the union experienced in the womb continues after birth until the process of individuation begins. But if this at-one-ness with the mother – our first experience of unity on the earth plane – does not function 'well enough', then we experience a sense of abandonment.

For others, the mother may be over-identified with the child, unable or unwilling to see it as anything other than an extension of herself. Then the child experiences engulfment, a sense of being swallowed up so that it is hard for him to develop his individuality.

Both these experiences can affect future relationships. The first transition on the earth plane – birth, and the first relationship with the mother – are powerful. Because it is at a pre-verbal and pre-conceptual stage, the child has no means of making sense of what happens, it simply absorbs it in the fabric of its being and responds from there in later relationships. Psychotherapy sometimes known as 'the talking cure' can help in giving voice to early experiences at a later date, in order that the adult may integrate them into the personality. We then have a choice about how we respond, instead of letting our unconscious do the talking.

In a way, abandonment in the psychological sense mirrors the separation the soul has just experienced in leaving behind soul plane unity. Added to this, a baby cannot survive physically without external help for several years. These two things give abandonment an existential aspect; the soul/baby feels its very survival is threatened.

Similarly when parents do not acknowledge the child's individuality but see him as a part of themselves, the child feels threatened at a survival level.

Because they are initially unconscious, these strands are acted out in adult relationships. The child who experienced abandonment fears being abandoned again, and develops behaviours to ensure that doesn't happen. Such a person may become demanding, manipulative and critical, or conversely placating, in order to keep a partner. This behavior may well have the opposite effect, driving potential partners away. Or alternatively, the individual with abandonment issues may habitually end a relationship first, to prevent the partner having a chance of 'abandoning' them.

The child who experienced engulfment has an exaggerated need for freedom within relationships, in order to cope with their fear of losing their individuality. In reality, because adults – parents included – are complex beings, we often wind up having both strands to deal with at different times or in different relationships.

The resulting fear – which links early psychological abandonment and engulfment – is fear of intimacy, a crucial factor in how we develop spiritually and psychologically. Both strands have the effect of pushing partners away, seeming to affirm the original problem and often leading to the same difficulties in subsequent relationships, until something provides a trigger to look more deeply.

The external difficulties we experience give indications of and ways of working through our internal conflicts. The trigger may be meeting a particular person, a partner or therapist, a colleague, friend or family member, at a time when we are ready to change.

Intimacy is an emotional and/or physical approximation of spiritual contact or exchange. It can happen in a moment, in eye contact and recognition, or can take years of getting to know someone before we feel relaxed and safe enough to allow intimate exchanges to happen. Intimacy has a feeling – for both people – of openness, of heart-contact, of soul-contact, an unconditional deep exchange. It can happen in friendship, in partnerships, in sexual contact and in helping relationships. Barriers and defences fall away, and we experience each other in all our vulnerabilities and in all our beauty. Intimacy flows between two people in a way that takes into account both individuals as well as the sense of themselves as a partnership – whether for a moment or a lifetime.

Intimacy is not losing a sense of self, it is rather enhancing it. We no longer need someone to prove their love so that we don't fear abandonment, and we no longer need to put distance between ourselves and the other person in order to prevent them overwhelming us. Intimacy nourishes us and strengthens us, and we get a sense of that soul contact which is our birthright as spiritual beings in physical bodies.

Intimacy requires a condition of openness and for that to operate, we need to be strong in ourselves, in our sense of self. Before we reach that strength, there are many people along the way who are needy, who will take strength from whatever source they can find. These people leech energy from us, drain us if we remain open on demand. Just as our parents protected us in babyhood by providing the boundaries, we need to develop our own boundaries and protection.

Usually, people who drain us are not aware they are doing it; at a conscious level they do not intend to take from us. Similarly, we will have developed our own protection at an unconscious level as we've grown and developed as individuals away from our parents. But in some cases, our defences and protection fail, maybe through sickness or emotional vulnerability, or through heightened sensitivity, and we need to make conscious the way we deal with protection and boundaries. Often the first indication that our defences have failed is when we become so depleted, we have trouble coping in our lives. This is where the work we have done on our energetic system can start to be useful.

The psychic space which surrounds each of us is the aura, see Diagram 10, the egg-shaped individual energy field. It interpenetrates the physical body and extends some distance away from us, depending on activity, state of well-being and level of our development. The edge of the aura in an ideal state is permeable, allowing other energies to come in, as well as letting through energies and responses from us. In this way we can tune in to the energy fields of other people, plants, animals and the universal energy field which permeates our earth plane.

If we are in good psychological, spiritual and physical health, these exchanges happen automatically with no difficulty. We allow the exchanges at an unconscious level, controlled by the subtle systems in our spiritual and physical bodies. When we find we are being drained by a person or situation it is a sign that we are giving out more than we are replenishing. If we can identify when this happens, we can prepare in advance, but until then it is better to start taking precautions when going out of the home.

Exercise for Protection of your Personal Boundaries

It is wise, as you continue with your evolving awareness and development, to have a daily spiritual routine, just as you shower, clean your teeth etc for your physical well-being.

A simple way to prevent draining or intrusion is visualisation, a method which speaks to the unconscious in images, a language it understands. This exercise works to prevent anyone draining you or overwhelming you with their presence or needs.

In a quiet place where you will be undisturbed, sit relaxed and symmetrically, without crossing legs or arms. Visualise yourself putting on a cloak of light or surrounded by an egg-shaped aura of light. You may begin to see swirling colours within the egg shape, all with the quality of sunlight. See how far your aura extends away from you. The edge of the aura is like the shell of the egg, and the permeability is under your conscious control. Keep it in your mind that you will give out only what is right for you, no more and no less. You choose what you let in. You need to remember to balance what you give out by consciously taking time to restore your energies, whether that is by sleeping, walking, being alone, talking with like-minded people, music, whatever suits you.

You can minimise the access people have to your energy by becoming aware of your personal space. Your aura ebbs and flows around you; anyone standing within it can more easily absorb energy from you. Take a step back if you feel it happening, choose a seating arrangement that prevents it occurring, do whatever you can to protect yourself until you get into the habit of strengthening your aura.

Understanding these simple procedures and coming to terms with intimacy are big steps along the way of spiritual and psychological growth. You can learn to be aware of changes in your aura, in how it extends and retracts in different situations.

If, after working with these practices, you still feel particularly fatigued or stressed after an occasion or encounter, you can try 'aura stroking'. Imagine the edge of your aura to be like a cat's fur, or iron filings, both of which like to be 'stroked' in a certain direction. Starting at the top of your head, at a distance which feels comfortable, stroke downwards with open palms, not touching the body, aiming to stroke the edge of the aura. Continue as far as you are able to reach, all around your body, short or long strokes, until you reach your feet. Be aware as you finish at the feet that you are grounding yourself, sensing the ground beneath you. If you have a friend you trust who can do this for you, that would be beneficial, reaching more of the areas it is difficult to reach on your own. With practice, this can feel calming as your aura has a chance to recover, with everything balanced.

While you are learning how to protect and calm your aura, you could visual an egg of silver or white light around the edges of your aura. Practice this at the end of your exercises, and each time you go out, or go into a situation you find potentially difficult. It will not only protect you but give you an energy boost as well, enabling you to carry light and energy with you. If you find it difficult to visualise an egg shape, imagine wrapping yourself in a cloak of white light. This is a good practice to include in your daily routine.

Chapter 9
Living with Spirit

*Development of spiritual consciousness; the stages of
psychological life; the stages of spiritual life.*

Much has been written in so-called New Age writings about the
advisability of parents being open to their children's psychic or
spiritual awareness. And indeed this is reasonable advice. But it
is not the whole picture.

A number of people who channel wisdom from sources with a
wider perspective than our own say that some children being
born today are more open, more advanced spiritually, and that
they need special help and understanding to develop their gifts.
And again, this is not an unreasonable hypothesis. But both
these statements can leave parents, who are trying to be
spiritually aware with and for their children, feeling inadequate.

The important attribute of all parenting is that parents try to
match their children's needs *without expectation*. Gone are the
days when parents assume their children will follow their fathers
and become accountants or lawyers, joiners or farmers. But
subtle expectations inevitably abound, and people following
their own spiritual path may want or expect their children to do
the same. Indeed, it is very hard as a parent on a spiritual path to
see their children apparently living a very mundane or even
hedonistic life. Unless the child is damaging himself, the key is
not to judge; none of us can know the path another is taking,
what their soul learning plan involves. Nor can we assess what
is spiritual and what is not, on behalf of another. Viewed one
way, the entire path we take is spiritual, it is all part of our
learning.

Openness is the best attitude here. If parents can be open to their children's development, encouraging when they show interest or aptitude, and offer a wide variety of opportunities and experiences, then that is good parenting. By being open, parents also give an example to their children, showing acceptance and a positive response to others. It sounds simple but getting a 'good enough' balance is not so easy. It takes work, self-awareness and understanding. And this is not the same as indulging the child's every whim; they still need guidance to prepare them for the world.

Watching for those subtle expectations, setting aside one's own hopes and dreams for the child, is challenging; naturally we want what we consider 'the best' for our children. Balancing guidance and encouragement so that it does not force the child into an unsuitable way of life is a tricky task. And treading the fine line between spoiling the child by giving in to all its wants and spotting the crucial needs, is a constant endeavour. No wonder all parents make mistakes, but most of us do the job 'well enough'. This highlights the value of each person working on their own spiritual awareness in order to contribute to the common pool of humanity's development, and to set a 'good enough' example for their children. It takes a lot of alertness, discernment and maturity to set aside personal preferences for the sake of another.

We so want our children to have advantages and perhaps the understanding we didn't have, to skip the hard parts, the opposition or blocking, or to start a rung up the ladder instead of at the bottom. Each individual's experience has to be theirs, and theirs alone. Parents cannot know the conditions their child's soul needs, however much they want to. It is, after all, hard enough to understand the conditions needed for one's own soul to flourish. Forcing or rushing development of incipient spiritual or psychic interests and abilities can be just as damaging as ignoring them. Every one of us, child or adult, needs to move at our own and no one else's pace.

It is true that some very young children are more open to other levels and may experience things that are beyond the experience of the parents. Parents can still guide the child, study books or find reputable help from someone experienced and if possible, recommended. Parents are not the only teachers; to be truly open is to know one's personal limits and to seek appropriate help when challenged beyond that.

And sometimes children are teachers to their parents. Parents and children can be fellow travellers, making a journey of discovery together, even while parents maintain boundaries (on all levels) for both themselves and their children. In this case especially, but it is also true for all children, a child is still a child, however much he seems to teach and share, and has a child's needs for emotional, psychological and spiritual care. A child needs to play, to rough and tumble, watch tv, mix with other kids on a fun level and simply have time to 'chill' in their own way.

Much publicised are the children who remember a past life, but these are rare and it is not usual, as we have seen in earlier chapters, to remember what we have left behind. There is enough to cope with in this incarnation, without myriad feelings and impressions from another. But a child who does show signs of remembering needs gentle help, not forcing, neither disbelieving nor over-encouragement. Aim at normalizing the situation while holding in mind the special kinds of protection needed by such a child. Accepting as normal or usual a child's burgeoning spiritual awareness is the best – and safest – policy, because that is exactly what it is – normal, whether or not it coincides with a parent's view. Until the personality is sufficiently formed and strong enough, acceptance and boundaries are priceless gifts from parent to child. It is worth repeating, this does not mean giving in to a child's every whim. It involves guidance as they increase their contact with life outside the home. Other, and maybe the biggest gifts we can give our child, are the tools to deal with everyday life. Practical skills, the ability to look after oneself, decision making, or having to fit in to school or office even when it seems to go against what the child wants. Wants and needs are different, but we all need to be able to live in the world.

So spiritual consciousness may be already active in a child. Or it may be that during the process of leaving behind memory of the soul plane, the child lost the idea of spirit too. But no one loses their connection to spirit or to other souls. It is simply that awareness of it needs to be reactivated, each individually and in our own time.

As well as the personality forming and surrounding the soul, events in childhood build up layers of protection or defence. If the childhood is particularly traumatic, thick layers of scar tissue build in the personality, making soul contact and response difficult. See Chapter 4. But the condition of being on earth means that everything is in a state of continual change, and the soul who wants to grow will discover ways of breaking down the scar tissue and finding a way through. It is a process best taken slowly and with dedication; little and often rather than sudden intense forays into metaphysical studies and activities. It is tempting in the first flush of enthusiasm at the beginning of this journey, to rush ahead. Resist it! There is a phrase which is apt here: Be Gentle with Yourself.

Many activities help this process; creativity of all kinds: writing, music – listening, singing or playing; painting, art – any form of beauty that touches the soul; nature – being outdoors, sensing the earth, the sea, contact with growing things, with pets, feeling awe at skyscapes and the stars can all touch the soul and begin healing and opening. Laughter and play/fun also contribute to healing certain chakras.

Creative visualisation and meditation, yoga, breathing exercises, t'ai chi and others are valuable aids in clearing energy blockages and keeping the mind and subtle energy channels clear, reducing stress and anxiety.

Sometimes it is a person who triggers opening or healing in us: an understanding teacher who observes and brings out the best in a child or adult; falling in love causes the heart to open like a flower, and soul response becomes a possibility; a friend, a kindred spirit, who recognises soul potential (although they may not call it by that name) and relates to you on the same wavelength; intimacy – that is deep contact and recognition of another being – is a soul contact. Diagram 5-a.

We see here two stages of spiritual life, that of the child and that of the parent, intertwining. These are specifics, parts of life that have been underestimated and abused and which now need to be brought into the light of understanding. Living a spiritual life is an everyday task. Working with the chakras is an important part of this development.

The general decline in formal religious life, churches emptier than in the past, has resulted in a decline in spiritual life or awareness for some people. But that isn't necessary. Each time we respond to someone with openness, or greet nature with an open heart, or think of someone with love …. all these and many more are small spiritual acts which make up our spiritual practice or life. Practice is a good word, it reminds us that however much progress we make, we still have to be aware and make the effort to practice what we believe. Recognising soul contact, however fleeting, is a major step. We can build on the small things by using meditation (and/or other things previously listed) to deepen our awareness of ourselves and the stillness within. Only in the stillness can awareness rise and become available to us. Too often in our busy world we lose ourselves in busy-ness, in doing rather than allowing time for being.

In Chapters 5 and 6 on the chakras, psychological development was discussed up to the age of 21. Developing the personality and learning to live in the world takes up that period for most people.

From age 21 to midlife, approximately another 21 years, the personality continues to refine as it lives in the world, forging a career, breaking away from the parents physically and geographically by leaving home, often undertaking commitments such as marriage and children. In many ways these are the years of greatest busy-ness and pressure, establishing oneself and one's family. If it can be done with spiritual awareness, so much the better. But for many, the world of work is ruthless, and trying to hold to principles of fairness, equality and respect alongside the cut and thrust, is difficult but not impossible. How does one manage to hold the thought that all are brothers and sisters in spirit when someone climbs the ladder by stepping on others? Or a colleague is promoted ahead of you when you have done all the 'right' things? And in personal life it is a challenge to hold these principles in the face of betrayal or divorce.

By mid-forties, many careers and families are established, and there can be a reaching out for other knowledge, for pursuing other interests, a small space for practicing ideals. For some, this time sees a resurgence in interests and beliefs not explored since teenage years. Psychologically, any unresolved issues from those years may also be revisited, an opportunity to sort out difficulties from a different perspective, that of maturity. The years around the mid-forties are essentially a time when physical, mental and emotional trials to be faced in the world and at home, a time for giving to the mundane world and to family. The individual is on the cusp of the third age, when the Self learns to live with the self.

Remember that these stages are flexible, sometimes overlapping. Therefore, these 21 year periods are somewhat arbitrary; we need to be flexible in our thinking so as not to limit ourselves and others by compartmentalising. With the increase in divorce and remarriage, these periods are changing. Often there has to be a re-establishment; two homes, two families to support instead of one, new relationships which need nurturing. For many, the forties have become a time reminiscent of their thirties in striving and busy-ness, and there can be an inevitable delay in opportunities for re-connecting to the things closest to the heart. In some ways, this can give people a second bite of the cherry, an extended time within the incarnation to come to terms with certain issues. And as we generally live longer than in the past, we have the time to do this.

For some, retirement age has become the subject of choice not prescription, and so the 'third age' psychologically and spiritually is also extended. By 60 or 65, usually children have left home, grandchildren are arriving, a way of life is established, and for many still-active people, a new way of life opens up. It may be through doing voluntary work for a charity, by acts of kindness to neighbours, or a new area of study. Often grandparents have a vital role to play in grandchild-minding when their adult children work. This is vital work, bringing patience and tolerance where busy striving lives fail to allow that for children. Being part of a young child's development, when you yourself have time to give, can be a most rewarding experience on both sides. Generally speaking, and in ideal circumstances, the third age is for living and developing more spiritually for those who are so minded.

A working life accumulates a lot of dross which weighs heavy. World-weariness, bitterness, cynicism can creep in during the working life, and the beginning of the third age or stage is a time for releasing this, letting go anything which holds back, anything which is negative or damaging to how you think and feel and are. It can be a time of re-discovery of one's basic needs, hopes and beliefs.

At this age, an awareness of the limited time of incarnation is developing. Friends and colleagues may get sick or die, bringing up ideas and feelings about one's own mortality. But because we are generally healthier than any older generation in our history, we have time and energy to put into searching – or consolidating our search – for a connection to spirit, to finally find out or consolidate who we are, and to deeply appreciate what it means to be spiritual beings in physical bodies. Again, if we have been adding meditation, visualisation exercises and other practices previously mentioned which aid awareness and well-being, we will feel the benefits at this time of life.

It is no coincidence that there is an increase in research into family history, for example. The leisure and mass resources to do this means we can see where we have come from as a prelude to finding ideas about how our lives have been lived, and where we might go next. Family traits and strengths can be understood to have helped shape us. The cycle of Life and Death – the eternal enigma – begins to come into focus.

To sum up, development encompassing both psychological and spiritual growth can be categorized in approximately three stages.

1. Learning: approximately first 21 years of life, exploration of who we are.
2. Putting into practice: approximately the next 40 years, moving out into the world, working, and giving out to the family.
3. Consolidation: last third of life, converting or transmuting knowledge and experience gained in life so far, into what might be called wisdom; giving to wider community, recognizing more deeply our spiritual selves.

All stages overlap and can interface, and the time each one lasts is variable. These are general guidelines.

Wisdom needs definition here. It is a condition or attribute stemming from accumulated knowledge, learning, skill, practice and experience which becomes more than the sum of its parts. The mind works with the heart to produce evaluations balanced in intellect and emotion. Wisdom is non-judgemental, is offered appropriately and free from any attachment to outcome, it is non-dogmatic and holds within itself deep respect for the timing and the path trodden by others.

Wisdom in elders was esteemed in tribal societies the world over, but in the west older people have too often become figures of fun, victims of crime, neglect and cruelty, and there is a general lack of understanding about what it means to be older and experienced. It is time to redress the balance, to respect, to nourish and be nourished by that unacknowledged wealth. But older people need to earn that respect, too; it is not an absolute right.

Chapter 10
Third Age

Towards androgyny – the balance of masculine and feminine energies within the individual; approaching the last transition of incarnation; reunion.

One of the biggest challenges we can face as individuals as well as collectively is how we use and balance masculine and feminine energies within ourselves, consciously or unconsciously. It should be noted that the earth plane is one of the lower planes where we can do this. On higher planes, there is no defined male and female, only individual beings, so our incarnation on the earth plane is an opportunity to develop the balance and understanding of these energies connected to our ideas of male and female, masculine and feminine.

I will not attempt to go into this deeply, there is much information if anyone wants to do that, but for the purpose of exploring our twin journeys, it deserves to be acknowledged.

Over centuries in our society, male and female roles became polarized and stereotyped. In recent years we have been moving away from the paternalistic society of centuries. The Women's Movement arose to try to achieve for women the same levels of freedom and opportunity enjoyed by men, and to end many forms of repression. As a result, some women have been able to liberate their masculine energy, and some men have started to experience and use their feminine energy free from fear of ridicule. Child, home care and financial responsibility are shared in many families, a blend of both energies.

It has been the butt of jokes to ridicule those who chose to express energy not inherent in the gender of an individual, eg. as women in a man's world had to over-emphasise their masculine energy while hiding (to some extent) their feminine energy. The task now is to balance these masculine and feminine energies both externally and internally i.e. in society and within ourselves. Our aim is co-operation between the sexes, instead of competition. It is happening but maybe even more awareness of it would help.

Traditionally, repression of both women and men is caused by polarization of our ideas about what is masculine and what is feminine. Some examples, and you will also have your own ideas.

traditional stereotypes:

Masculine	*Feminine*
initiating	passivity
aggression	compliance
dominance	dependence
hardness	softness
logic, reason	emotion, intuition
structure	fluidity
ambition	contentment
material provider	provider of tenderness, nurture

If we can demonstrate qualities from all parts of the spectrum in appropriate situations, we are well on the way to integrating these energies. Society is struggling on many fronts, which affects how easily it can adapt, though change is already happening. The speed with which technology has and continues to change our working and home lives is phenomenal. We need to continue to develop a more balanced outlet both at work and at home for men and women to express different sides of themselves. Outward expression consolidates internal change. Paternity leave is an obvious aspect of helping that balance. Women as corporate heads in commerce is another, but there are many subtle changes in the way we live, dress, play and relate. Such changes have to filter right through society and become the norm.

Closely linked to these changes are ideas about how we express our sexuality. Part of the change in society has been more openness and acceptance about LGBT – lesbian, gay, bisexual and transgender – a term which came into use around the late 1980's. Even within this area, stereotypes arose and were difficult to uproot in common usage. The 'effeminate homosexual', the 'butch lesbian', camp expressions in fashion and interests were all held up to ridicule. It has taken time to settle so that more facets of LGBT are accepted. Transgender refers not only to sexual orientation, but to gender non-conforming too. We need freedom, acceptance and inclusion to express all aspects of our personality, sexuality and gender orientation.

Bisexuality is the term traditionally used to describe people who have sexual partners of both sexes. Some psychologists would include those people who have an inclination to have partners of both sexes, but who in their lives remain with one sex, suggesting that bisexuality is a psychological factor in the make-up of the personality. However you wish to define it, there is a vital component to this inclination or behaviour – the desire or need to express energies in non-stereotypical ways. See Appendix 1 for a recent definition of how 'gender' and 'sex' are used.

There was a phase when it became 'fashionable' to display overt lesbian behaviour, and there is a perceived increase in or acceptance of bisexuality. There is a psycho-spiritual aspect to all this behaviour, beyond the personal, beyond the apparent frivolity of fashion.

In those people influenced by stereotypical masculinity and femininity, there is often one repressed or hidden aspect. To liberate and integrate this aspect, society and individuals have been making the changes to stereotypes already mentioned. The harmonious co-existence of the masculine and feminine within one person, the aim of this re-balancing, is called androgyny. Traditionally androgyny referred to the state of being neither masculine nor feminine, but as our understanding grows, it can also refer to the combination of masculine and feminine characteristics. See Appendix 1.

Androgyny is a universal image, by definition unconscious but appearing in stories the world over that helps bring it to consciousness. Developing our own awareness of the masculine and feminine energies within so we may, by choice, use them appropriately in different situations, is to develop our internal androgyne.

As always on the earth plane, we express this through the personality. Our longing for a partner with whom we might share our life, with whom we can 'be one' or 'be at one' is part of the search for our own wholeness. We believe the longed-for person will make us feel complete.

Balancing the way we express the masculine and feminine energies within us, whatever our sexual or gender orientation and without extremes of either machismo or dependency, is androgyny and it leads to wholeness. Once enough of us recognise our wholeness and internal unity, we may begin to express it in the outer world. Old stereotypes and polarisations will fade out. When enough people approach this stage on an individual level, society, as a whole, will make a more definite and lasting shift towards balance.

We live in times where this is possible. We each have a contribution to make; bringing up our children with open expectation, watching over grandchildren, developing ourselves, helping others. It is inevitable that, as history shows, there is usually a swing towards an extreme before balance in achieved. It is a third-stage task to consolidate all we can before we face the last great transition of this incarnation, death.

NOTE: Although we may identify with a particular gender or sex in this lifetime, during many incarnations we will all have experience of different genders and sexuality.

Chapter 11
Preparing for the Last Transition

We have briefly mentioned the increasing awareness that this incarnation is drawing to a close, prompted by ageing, by personal ill health or the death of our contemporaries. Some people prepare for death: making wills, decluttering their home, tidying personal papers, while others put it on the back burner, always meaning to do something about it – someday. It is not necessary to be morbid or to dwell on death, but some preparation helps, and not only on the practical level. I am referring here to death through what might be termed natural causes, old age or illness, when there is some awareness that death may be close. Other types of death, accidental and premature etc. will be discussed in the next chapter.

There is a hackneyed question people ask each other at certain times, when they are reminded of endings: how would you spend your last day on earth? It elicits frivolous as well as serious answers. The question would be better asked: what are you doing to prepare for moving on from this earth plane? Death is not a sudden stopping, it is part of a process of transition from living in a physical body, letting that go, moving back to living wholly in spirit. Just as at birth, there is (generally speaking) a moving closer to that moment of transition over a period, so the physical body, in old age or illness is slowly let go.

The Personality, the Body and the Soul will all have different requirements in the preparation for dying. Although requirements will overlap, each aspect needs attention, both by the person dying and by the carers around that person. Many of us get stuck in one or other of the aspects, focusing on that almost entirely, and failing to give attention to the others. It is easy, for example, to concentrate on the needs of the failing physical body. It is worth looking at each in general terms.

Personality

The personality has to deal with many – often difficult – aspects such as letting go of emotional ties, what it means to be old, or dependent again, fears and anxiety around the process of illness/old age/dying. Some people fear the manner of death, fearing illness and frailty. Others fear death itself as the great unknown and would cling on to life at any cost. The prospect of losing family and friends, a sense of what is perceived as reality, and apparently the entire life as it has been known, is terrifying for some.

Old fears can become exaggerated, out of perspective, in the elderly. And there are often practical fears in terms of finance and the reality of coping.

A person who has dependents may have particular difficulties when faced with dying. How do you leave a loved one who relies on you? If your loved one doesn't want to let you go, how do you – firmly and lovingly – say that you must leave? There are remarkable stories about the dying hanging on to life for days or weeks, because their family finds it impossible to think of being without them, or refuses to accept the reality of their decline. Many workers with the dying report that an individual finally passes just as the loved ones leave the room for a few minutes. It is as if they take the moment when it will least distress the loved one, or when they don't feel held back from passing on.

Sometimes a level of serenity in the personality comes naturally, with the acceptance of all one has seen, been and done. When serenity and acceptance permeate the personality, the soul is also affected, ultimately easing the transition. Work we have done in years past towards understanding our spiritual journey will help this process.

Sometimes there are left-over threads of life to deal with; an estranged family member to contact, a journey dreamed of but never made. Commonly we call this our bucket list. Regret, guilt, forgiveness and the need for forgiveness may all come into the mind at this time. People move in smaller circles, perhaps staying closer to home, seeing fewer new people, wanting visitors to come to them instead of making trips themselves.

At this time there is often an urge to make sense of one's life, understand what will continue after death. Telling family stories, sharing both the laughter and tears, can be a remarkable learning and release for speaker and listener alike. Everyone needs to know, at the level of the personality, that they have mattered in some way to someone. But for some, all of this can happen without words. There is a 'being-ness' about the dying process that is perhaps more important than all the 'doing' and talking. Being with a person coming to the end of their earthly life is a wonderful gift, and not all of us think about giving it.

All these things have something in common – an awareness (verbalised or not) that this incarnation is drawing to a close.

Body

The physical body as it ages needs extra care, more time taken to keep it comfortable and in optimum working order according to age and health conditions.

How we view the body will influence the way we deal with the physical aspect of coming closer to dying. Some people manage to think of the body as 'purely mechanical' and can almost ignore discomfort and limitations, or at least live with them. Others need help and support to get the most from bodies which can no longer perform as they did, bodies that are increasingly frail.

The body and emotions are inextricably linked in humans. We come to this existence as beings physically dependent entirely on another for survival, and often at the end of life, there is a return to this condition. The nature of early transitions in our life, the quality of nurturing and care, may still affect how we deal with this last dependence. For example, if we learned not to trust others to give us the care we needed when we were vulnerable babies, we may go on to lead lives of independence, hiding our fear, while believing we must do everything for ourselves. For these people, dependence late in life is very hard.

If the body is as comfortable as we can make it, and we can gain an acceptance that it has limitations or takes more time than previously, then we can develop some equanimity which frees us to deal with other aspects.

Soul

The soul is preparing to leave the earth plane and return to the soul plane, with all its differing conditions and vibrations. It is a journey. How would you prepare for a journey? Perhaps finding information about the journey is important to you. Or building up your strength of mind or body. If you have been aware of spirit in your lifetime, you will instinctively have some thoughts about your needs.

The soul has been living on the earth plane with its heavy vibrations, protected by a personality and a physical body. It is about to leave those behind and enter the lighter soul plane once more. So there is a certain amount of shedding – some things become less important as we become aware of dying. Some things take on new, even urgent, importance. Bringing these thoughts to awareness helps us to know how we can best prepare. We can strengthen the soul and our soul connection in many ways: giving and receiving love, music or art which moves us, the sea, the countryside, reading our favourite texts which speak to us of spirit or unity. Many people find they need extra quiet time during this process, something which is not always readily available as relatives and friends want to visit, or in some cases of illness, because of medical procedures at all hours. Hard as it is, because we want to meet others' needs too in this process of dying, it is right to find the quiet time we need to ease our progress.

Hospices are places of light and healing where consideration is given to all aspects of dying, recognising it as a physical, psychological and spiritual transition. Counsellors are on hand if needed, medication to reduce pain levels, and perhaps above all, a place of freedom where death is acknowledged and spoken of, if desired – something that is often difficult in family situations.

Exercise

Just as it was a good idea to recount our birth story and to have it witnessed, it is a good idea towards the end of this incarnation to have a review of our life, either written down or verbal. It does not have to be formal, eg. looking through photograph albums, even sketching according to our need. Be creative, review in whatever way feels comfortable. Reviewing life gives opportunities to revisit parts as memories arise and want to be added, and we may feel the need to have parts of it witnessed, just as with the birth story. This is an affirmation of a life lived.

Chapter 12
Death and After
The last transition of incarnation, and reunion

The process of dying

Those who work with the terminally ill frequently report a gradual distancing or withdrawing in the dying person. They relate to those around, to family and friends, but something is changing almost indefinably. At the same time, those who have led a life with awareness of spiritual consciousness may start to sense other dimensions, perhaps other beings. Just as at birth, when the soul wishing to incarnate was guided and shepherded to its conception, so at death discarnate beings come close to receive and guide again, back to the unity of the soul plane.

Time as we know it here on earth has no relevance on the soul plane, and so in the processes of approaching death, time has little meaning. For one person, the distancing can be in a few moments, for others, it can happen over months.

In terms of the sick or elderly, physical weakness occurs of course, as the body starts to shut down. The senses become blurred; outlines but not details may be perceived, light but not shape, for example. Some teachings say that hearing is the last sense to close down, and given that we now have some evidence towards the belief that the foetus/soul in the womb responds to sound, it may be that the soul withdrawing from the earth plane is also sensitive to sound until the last moment of breath. Certainly, family and carers may continue to speak or read softly and lovingly to the dying person, in a way which does not hinder their journey, using texts or music that have been loved during the lifetime.

There are many reports of near-death experience suffered during trauma. A common theme is a bright light which draws the transitioning soul onwards. Many people have said they saw or heard a loved one greeting them. Various people have tried to discredit these reports by offering scientific explanations which make these phenomena seem ridiculous. But it remains a strong conviction in those who experience the light that it is a positive moving forward which they wish to follow. Some feel that it is their choice whether to follow or not, whether it is their time to leave or not.

Traditional religious teachings have positive expectations about what happens after death, at least have names for the places and stages, and some understanding of what happens at each stage. It is a comfort for those who need that, during a potentially frightening, bewildering or painful transition.

Some say that we will see whatever we expect to see when we die, that we will experience whatever aspects are in our minds. If we expect nothingness, we will experience a kind of limbo. But whatever the personal belief, there is never the 'snuffing out' that is often part of the atheistic belief system. All souls continue to move on, in their different ways.

Part of the preparation is to find out what we need, perhaps read as many variations on the theme as we can until we find a scenario resting in our minds that seems right. It may be a combination of teachings, and that's ok. During the preparation we will be coming to terms with the process of dying and gaining acceptance.

Those who have used the third age to explore and continue their spiritual journeys, are more likely to move with grace and consideration, acceptance and love towards the transition, minimising any fear or sadness.

The drawing closer to the spirit world can take the form of dreams, increasing in vividness, in feeling content. Or it can take the form of daydreams, meditations, prayers or musings, so that we bring back, on waking to everyday reality, a sense of unity that is lacking in life. Often a feeling of serenity follows these processes.

And so death becomes for some people a kind of slipping away. One day in the dream, daydream or musing they just go a step further and don't return to the everyday reality they knew.

Of course, we have only referred to death from illness or old age. Deaths by accident or sudden trauma have different requirements. The person may seem catapulted forward into death, with no preparation and no warning. Most religions have special prayers for such events, to ease the shock and suffering of the newly-dead. For they are in shock, just as anyone would be if the physical body survived an accident or trauma.

After an accident, the physical body may be, bruised, injured, the mind shocked and disorientated. In death, the physical body may be left behind but the soul may suffer the equivalent of these conditions. Just as on earth, nurses and doctors are trained to take care of the injured, so specially trained beings from the soul plane will come close to our dimension to receive and help the newly-dead who are in shock as they make the transition to the soul plane.

At times of major loss of life such as multiple crashes, disasters or war, many of these beings come to help and guide, so that no soul is left to suffer and wander alone. Advanced souls who are still incarnate but have the skills may also help, making the mental journey from the earth plane to a place approaching the spirit plane in order to aid those in shock.

Suicide is another type of death with all its pain and suffering, and even stigmas. Again, there will be beings who have a special understanding of suicide, there to counsel, console and help the newly passed over soul. There is no judgement, just understanding and compassion.

In Chapter 1, another kind of death was mentioned, that of terminations or still-born babies. The souls who came close to the earth plane in this way will be looked with the same care, with helpers and counsellors. Their experience in being close to the parents and the earth plane will help them in future incarnations, as well as increasing the understanding of the group of souls of which they are a part. Sadly, society doesn't always allow grieving for such deaths in the same way as for other deaths. It is important to find ways of expressing grief and acknowledging the soul who came close. Each individual may find a way to do this, perhaps with a small private ritual, a written piece. It may seem important to name the child, anything which recognises the grief and the soul.

Immediately after death, there may be a stay in what have been called the Halls of Healing for a recovery period. With no concept of time as we know it, there is no pressure to move on or hurry to 'get well'. In the next stage, the newly returned soul meets with tutors or counsellors in the same way it met advisors at the start of this incarnation. In our physical terms, there would be a de-briefing, but with our limited senses we can have little concept of the way the exchange takes place at soul-to-soul level. What we have done with our lives, how we have lived them, our experiences and learning are all assessed by ourselves, with help, and passed into the greater collective knowledge and understanding of our soul family. No one 'judges' except ourselves. We are the sternest critic of our lives, and the soul exists in such a way that we would not let ourselves off lightly, or make excuses, but neither would we harbour guilt. Compassion, understanding, and wisdom are all part of this process.

It is ultimately hard to leave behind someone you love, partners, children, friends. A period of adjustment is needed to let the strands of the ties of personality fall away. The soul loosens all the ties and pulls of emotional relationships. Emotions such as desire, anger, regret, guilt fall away. Soul connections of course will remain, as well as familial love that has developed. A person who loved unconditionally on the earth plane can continue to 'watch over' the loved ones from their new plane.

There is a clarity, an awareness such as we might have glimpsed in meditation or in dreams. And there is the joy of reunion. Once again existing with souls in unity undreamed of and barely perceived as yet on the earth plane. It nourishes us as we give ourselves to the unity.

The process is cyclical. There will be recuperation and further learning to help in future incarnations. In due course, our helpers and advisors will meet with us again, to help us assess and make choices, to work out conditions for another incarnation, and another cycle will begin.

There are many books written about grief and mourning, and indeed it is an important process. But it is also important for the surviving family members to start the letting go process with the person dying, where this is appropriate for both parties. Sharing memories and recollections of earlier life, but also acknowledgements, finding out what they need in the dying process, what their wishes are for their body and estate after death, and saying goodbyes are all valuable things to do. Sometimes the dying person needs recognition from the family that it is ok to let go. Obviously, the family needs to show great sensitivity in such a case.

Those close to a dying person can offer many kinds of help and support. Some people may like to be spoken to or read to, even as they die or as an aid to the process of passing over to the next stage of existence. Some like music, others like silence. Often the dying person is conscious of the grief of their families and friends, and they don't like to ask for anything, or speak of their real feelings or fears to avoid any further upset. But a shared process can be a wonderful gift on both sides, if we do not let fear or sadness hold us back.

For those of us left behind, there will be the pain of physical parting, the sorrow of a loved and loving presence no longer in our daily lives, but that should not stop us daring to share the last great incarnational experience of this personality and soul.

Appendix 1
Definitions
As used in this book.

Androgyny
The balance of masculine and feminine energies within the indiviual.

Aura
The energy field surrounding, interpenetrating and extending beyond the human body.

Birth Story
'birth story' is used throughout to indicate the pre-natal history and birth experience, whether real or imagined, of the individual. Seen by Sensitives to be full of colours, some colours stemming from the chakras.

Chakra
Chakras are centres or points of energy with the energy field, called the Aura, surrounding the body. Fuller explanation appears in Chapter 5.

Counselling and Therapy
"The therapist can interpret, advise, provide the emotional acceptance and support that nurtures personal growth, and above all, he can listen. I do not mean that he can simply hear the other, but that he will listen *actively* and purposefully, responding with . . . . the personal vulnerability of his own trembling self. This listening is that which will facilitate the patient's telling of his tale, the telling that can set him free."
– *Sheldon Kopp, American Jungian Analyst.*

Gender generally refers to those roles, functions and identities often developed in response to society, family norms, peers, education, even media etc. See also 'sex'.

Incarnation
The span of the individuals time on the earth plane, from Birth to Death.

Individuation

Swiss Psychologist Carl Gustav Jung thought that individuation belongs to the second half of life, and is the process by which a person becomes a psychological individual.
The process of individual self-development comes out of personality growth and understanding.

My own observations and experience, both personal and with clients, lead me to believe that individuation can and does begin much earlier, and that there is a natural flowing from personality development and refinement into the process of integration leading to wholeness. The processes may inter-weave, the stages ebbing and flowing. Some people come to it in a much more conscious way than others.

Karma
Commonly thought of as Cause and Effects, often with a negative slant. It is far more than that.
Karma refers to the natural law concerning our voluntary acts, speech and thoughts, and their effects. We build up positive or negative karma according to the kind of lives we live, how we treat other people. The effects of karma may be lived out in different lifetimes, and each life does not have to resolve every effect from past lives.

Personality and its role

The personality is a collection of traits and characteristic ways of behaving, thinking, feeling and responding. This forms around a soul for the duration of its incarnation. The personality is formed from the essence of the soul and its past experience, from parental genes, and according to conditions obtaining during its development. Its role is to protect the soul from the harsh vibrations of the earth plane, and to allow the soul to take part in life here. It allows the soul to perceive, experience and participate in experiences which are unique to this plane of existence. Such experiences may be integrated to make personality formation an on-going process of refinement.

Plane

After the earth plane, there are other more subtle levels of experience. Ram Dass describes them "as a set of vibrations or frequencies, that which is beyond the beyond."

Reincarnation

The process of being born again on the earth plane.

Self: (upper case 'S') The Soul or animating force.

self: (with a lower case 's'): The ego or personality.

Sensitive

A person who perceives beyond the physical.

Sex

Tends to refer to biological differences.
'Sex' and 'gender' are often used interchangeably, despite coming to mean different things.

Soul

The animating force, the on-going eternal part of human consciousness, a spark of Spirit.

Soul plane or Heaven, Higher Plane

A word much bandied about, misused, misunderstood. In this text I use it to mean a level where there is an awareness of the Spirit, where the soul is free from physical and emotional ties.

Spirit – God: universal everlasting eternal undying, Source, Supreme Being.

Spiritual

Oxford Dictionary: relating to or affecting the human spirit. In this text, used to mean an awareness of another level of consciousness relating to Spirit.

Synchronicity

Swiss Psychologist Carl Gustav Jung coined the term synchronicity to signify "the simultaneous occurrence of two meaningful but not causally connected events," but which have a combined significance.

Script Theory in Transactional Analysis
Wiki:
a psychological theory which posits that human behaviour largely falls into patterns called "scripts" because they function analogously to the way a written script does, by providing a program for action.

Transgender refers not only to sexual orientation, but to gender non-conforming.
"The quality or state of being neither specifically feminine or

113

masculine: the combination of feminine and masculine characteristics: the quality or state of being androgynous."
– *Merriam Webster Dictionary.*

Addition to Appendix 2

PERCIVAL GILBERT MEDD (Gil) is a Psychologist from Morpeth, Northumberland. Born August 1941. Lecturer at University of Newcastle.

consultant, working as a channel for guidance from Gildas – her well-known discarnate Guide, running groups in the UK and Germany and a correspondence course in spiritual growth.

Barbara Somers and Ian Gordon Brown founded the Centre for Transpersonal Psychology in 1973.

Barbara Somers (1929-2013) was born in London, a psychological counsellor, therapist and workshop leader, with a Jungian background.

Ian Gordon-Brown (1925-1996) was born in Quetta (now in Pakistan). He was a consultant psychologist and psychotherapist in private practice.

Books:

References for the Birth Story and Personal Myth

Jean Shinoda Bolen, M.D. [1994]   Crossing to Avalon
J.C. Cooper [1983]   Fairy Tales: Allegories of the Inner Life
David Feinstein and Stanley Krippner [1988] Personal Mythology
Dr. Arthur Janov [1973]   The Feeling Child
[1990]   The New Primal Scream
Carl G. Jung [1961]   Memories, Dreams and Reflections
Rollo May [1991]   The Cry for Myth
Carol Pearson [1986]   Hero Within
Thomas M.D. Verny with John Kelly [1981] The Secret Life of the Unborn Child

Counselling and Communication

Diana Whitmore [1991]   Psychosynthesis Counselling in Action
Ian Stewart and Vann Joines [1987]   TA Today

116

Appendix 2 - Further reference: Books and Teachers

Teachers

Mary Cox M.Ed., TSTA(P) is a retired Teaching and Supervising Transactional Analyst (clinical) in private practice in Cumbria, England.

Ruth White is an accredited psychotherapist and maintains a private practice. She is also a spiritual consultant, working as a channel for guidance from Gildas – her well-known discarnate Guide, running groups in the UK and Germany and a correspondence course in spiritual growth.

Barbara Somers and Ian Gordon Brown founded the Centre for Transpersonal Psychology in 1973.

Barbara Somers (1929-2013) was born in London, a psychological counsellor, therapist and workshop leader, with a Jungian background.

Ian Gordon-Brown (1925-1996) was born in Quetta (now in Pakistan). He was a consultant psychologist and psychotherapist in private practice.

Books:

References for the Birth Story and Personal Myth

Jean Shinoda Bolen, M.D. [1994]   Crossing to Avalon
J.C. Cooper [1983]   Fairy Tales: Allegories of the Inner Life
David Feinstein and Stanley Krippner [1988]   Personal Mythology
Dr. Arthur Janov [1973]   The Feeling Child
[1990]   The New Primal Scream
Carl G. Jung [1961]   Memories, Dreams and Reflections
Rollo May [1991]   The Cry for Myth
Carol Pearson [1986]   Hero Within
Thomas M.D. Verny with John Kelly [1981] The Secret Life of the Unborn Child

Counselling and Communication

Diana Whitmore [1991]   Psychosynthesis Counselling in Action
Ian Stewart and Vann Joines [1987]   TA Today

116

Chakras

Ruth White   Working with the Chakras

Death and Dying

Elisabeth Kubler-Ross   Death and Dying

     Living with Death and Dying

Stephen Levine   Who dies?

     A year to live

Ram Dass   Walking each other Home

Sogyal Rinpoche   Tibetan Book of Living and Dying

General

Harvey Tordoff   O Lanoo!

John Welwood   Journey of the Heart

Jack Kornfield   Any of his books

Appendix 3

Table of Chakras and their correspondences

Chakra	Colours	Sense	Keywords
Root	Red, brown, mauve	Smell	Rootedness, Instinct, Physical Body
Sacral	Orange, amber, gold	Taste	Raw Emotional Energy, a Sense of Others, lymphatic system, Creativity.
Solar Plexus	Yellow, gold, rose	Sight	Personal Power, Drive, Initiating, Reason.

Heart	Green, rose, rose-amethyst	Touch	Love, Love of Others, Tenderness, Compassion, Non-judgementalism.
Throat	Blue, silver, turquoise	Hearing	Communication, Self-Expression, Responsibility.
Brow	Indigo, turquoise, mauve		Imagination, Inspiration, Insight, Self-realisation.
Crown	Violet, white, gold		Consciousness. Knowledge, Surrender, Soul

Sue Vickers Tordoff
Biography

I was born and raised in West Yorkshire, a county of glorious extremes of landscape and culture; dales, moorland, seascapes, industrial landscapes and architecture. Since my marriage in 1967 I have lived in several different counties, both north and south of Britain, as well as living for a year in Jamaica, W.I.

I first trained as a secretary and then audit clerk for a firm of chartered accountants, where I met my husband. We have one son. After working from home, in the 1970's I began to retrain as a counsellor and therapist, gradually adding skills in psycho-dynamic, person-centred and transpersonal perspectives, and also transactional analysis. In the 1980's, my own ill health led me to further investigate healing and eventually I trained as a healer, adding these skills to my practice.

For twenty years I worked in private practice and as a counsellor in a primary care team, also as a facilitator for groups learning counselling and healing. Later, I concentrated on writing and further studies.

Spiritual development and growth is a lifelong quest; I am a fellow traveller offering my understanding so far. This book is a distillation of my studies to date. It is a combination of knowledge, experience, and practice.

Professional Qualifications
1977-1995

I undertook studies in Psychology and Social Psychology at the University of Surrey, extra mural studies; Energy Healing with the National Federation of Spiritual Healers; Counselling with the Westminster Pastoral Foundation; Transactional Analysis including Personality Development with Mary Cox, Teaching and Supervising Transactional Analyst (clinical); and various aspects of Transpersonal Psychology at their centres in London and Edinburgh.

This led to Certificates and Diplomas in Counselling with Therapy with the 1) University of Newcastle, and 2) the Centre for Transpersonal Psychology, London; and 3) Le Plan International School of Healing, Provence, France.

Writing Credits

Over the years I published articles on counselling and related subjects, poems and short stories.
I also created and edited two literary websites for a decade: one a poetry ezine and one for a well-known poet.

Books:
Poetry: The Year of the Poem, 2020
   Sue-Scape, 2020
Fiction: [under the name Susie Alexander]
   The Shores of Myself, 2020
   The Wayshowers and Other Stories, 2021

Acknowledgements

First, I owe a great deal to my husband, for encouragement and patience particularly, and my son; together they support and hold me together with their love and caring. Other family members contribute almost daily to my enthusiasm for life. Many friends add to my continued well-being, those who help me find my Joy when I lose it, those who give me Courage, those whose own sense of Awe opens my eyes, and those who simply touch my heart with their love and generosity. Heather in particular believed in me when no one else did, least of all myself, the most valuable gift. And then of course there are my teachers, named elsewhere, who gave me knowledge and confidence, challenged me, picked me up when I faltered and generally had patience with my stumbling efforts. People come and go in our lives, and living a long life gives me an opportunity to put this in perspective, and to be glad of you all.